To Anne
With lo[illegible]
In good faith
[illegible]

Parousia

Love's Light

31-7-2019

Also by Francess

(Formerly Frances Smith- Williams)

Healing Poems for Positive Love

Book of Life

Lost Loves

Ultimate Healing Poems

Parousia

Love's Light

Parousia - Second Coming, Return or Presence of Christ
Love is always a positive state of being
Light; enlightenment for conscious understanding.

.

****

Parousia - Love's Light

Published January 2018

However these poems are inspired by a whole and positive spirit for the good of mankind. It is to this Whole Spirit of Love, namely Jesus Christ and ultimately the One God of Love who causes Love to become Whole in us that I give *thanks, credit and recognition to;* to the One who gives freely so I share freely. These poems are for sharing freely as you wish but please respect the years of writing and a life time of investment in my studies and working on self development to liberate the pain from unjust life experiences that has gone into the process of birthing these and other poems. I have bills to pay too.

Legal Notices

Through the use of poetry, the purpose of this book is to inspire new thought, entertain and educate readers on the subject matter covered.

The author assumes no responsibility or liability on the behalf of any purchaser or reader of this book and it is recommended that you consult your doctor if you have any health concerns or problems. Always seek medical attention if needed.

Cover Photograph taken by Francess in San Martino Monestery, Naples October 2017

ISBN-13: 978-1986606493

Dedicated to the return of Jesus Christ

****

To the One God of Love who causes Love to become whole in us for enlightenment for Positive Life energy in us for peace and a healing of *All Nations* with an abundance of fruits of His spirit made whole namely:

'Love, joy, peace, patience, kindness, goodness, faith, mildness, self control. Against such things there is no law'.
Galatians 5.22,

Freedom of the spirit of Love made whole in us in mind, body and spirit, the positive emotional states of being for Life Energy in us for trust, safety, peace and security for His Love to conquer stress and fear in us in mind, body and spirit. Love is a universal Positive force for good; The One God of Love and Light made whole in us, 'So Be Love' for God's Heavenly Kingdom to come down to Earth to dwell for peace and security on Earth for a healing for *'All Nations'*.

Amen, Ameen. Shalom, Namaste.

God Willing in English
Insh Allah in Arabic.
Shalom, Namaste
Maranatha

JHVH, YHWH: 'He who causes to become'
Yeshua, Jeshua. Jesus Christ; Anointed with
Whole Spirit of Love.
Allah: There is only One: Love
Abba: Father
'I shall prove to be what I prove to be' Exodus 3:14

His Love proved: Sealed.

****

2nd Timothy 3.

But know this, that in the last days critical times hard to deal with will be here. For men will be lovers of themselves, lovers of money, self assuming, haughty, blasphemers, disobedient to parents, unthankful, disloyal, having no natural affection, not open to any agreement, slanderers, without self control, fierce, without love of goodness, betrayers, headstrong, puffed up, lovers of pleasures rather than lovers of God, having a form of godly devotion but proving false to its power, and from these turn away…4:3 For there will be a period of time when they will not put up with the healthful teachings.

'Healthful teachings' God, God's Love is good for our psychological and emotional health and well being which is the positive energy that sustains our physical wellbeing by means of a positive mindset with Faith for Love and a healthy protective bio energy, the aura, the 'outer garments', or 'tent of God with mankind'. In my work I conclude God's Love is protecting the Love inside us by avoidance of stress which causes pain. God's Love creates natural endorphins in us for health and well being, it is why His teachings are worthy of total adherence and worship and honour in everyday life.
God's Love is the universal anti depressant.

Matthew 24:7 For nation will rise against nation and Kingdom against Kingdom and there will be food shortages and earthquakes in one place after another…22 In fact unless those days are cut short, no flesh would be saved., but on account of the chosen ones, those days will be cut short.

There will be many false Christ's and prophets - test every inspired expression. Test this work.

****

The Lord's Prayer

'Our Father who art in Heaven,
Hallowed be thy name,
Thy Kingdom Come,
Thy will be done on Earth as it is in Heaven,
give us this day our daily bread ...
and forgive us our trespasses
as we forgive those who trespass against us and
lead us not into temptation
and deliver us from evil
for thine is the Kingdom,
the power and the Glory
for ever and ever, Amen.

Revelation 21: New Jerusalem

Revelation 21:4 And God will wipe out every tear from their eyes, and death will be no more, neither will mourning nor outcry nor pain be anymore. The former things have passed away. 5 And the One seated on the throne said "look! I am making all things new". Also, he says "Write. Because these words are faithful and true"

21:11; It's radiance was like a most precious stone, as a jasper stone shinning crystal clear…

18 Now the structure of its wall was jasper, and the city was pure gold like clear glass. 19 The foundations of the city's wall were adorned with every sort of precious stone; The first foundation was jasper, the second sapphire, the third chalcedony, the fourth emerald,20 the fifth sardonyx, the sixth sardius, the seventh chrysolite, the eighth beryl, the ninth topaz, the tenth chrysoprase, the eleventh hyacinth, the twelfth amethyst. Also the twelve gates were twelve pearls, each one of the gates was made of one pearl. And the broad way of the city was pure gold, as transparent glass.

22 And I did not see a temple in it for JHVH God Almighty is its temple, also the Lamb. 23 And the city has no need of the sun nor of the moon to shine upon it, for the glory of God lighted it up and it's lamp was/is the Lamb. And the nations will walk by means of it's light and the kings of the earth will bring their glory to it.24 And its gates will not be closed at all by day, for night will not exist there 26 And they will bring the glory and the honour of the nations into it.
22.20 Yes; I am coming quickly Amen! Come, Lord Jesus.

I believe this is Faithful and True. Nothing added and nothing taken away, just concluded into a conscious universal language for Oneness of Love in mind, body and spirit.

****

12 x 12 = 144 thoughts made 0 (whole) in thought, word and deed: mind, body and spirit for cultivating the whole spirit of Love Anointed; namely Jesus Christ

144,000

Jasper Judah Courage	Sapphire Reuben Faith	Chalcedony Gad Happiness	Emerald Asher Peace	Sardonyx Naphtali Wrestlings understand	Sardius Manasseh Forgive	Chrysolite Simeon Hear	Beryl Levi Adherence	Topaz Issachar Reward	Chrysoprase Zebulun Tolerance	Hyacinth Joseph Trust	Amethyst Ben Truth
Sapphire Reuben Faith	Chalcedony Gad Happiness	Emerald Asher Peace	Sardonyx Naphtali Wrestlings understand	Sardius Manasseh Forgive	Chrysolite Simeon Hear	Beryl Levi Adherence	Topaz Issachar Reward	Chrysoprase Zebulun Tolerance	Hyacinth Joseph Trust	Amethyst Ben Truth	Jasper Judah Courage
Chalcedony Gad Happiness	Emerald Asher Peace	Sardonyx Naphtali Wrestlings understand	Sardius Manasseh Forgive	Chrysolite Simeon Hear	Beryl Levi Adherence	Topaz Issachar Reward	Chrysoprase Zebulun Tolerance	Hyacinth Joseph Trust	Amethyst Ben Truth	Jasper Judah Courage	Sapphire Reuben Faith
Emerald Asher Peace	Sardonyx Naphtali Wrestlings understand	Sardius Manasseh Forgive	Chrysolite Simeon Hear	Beryl Levi Adherence	Topaz Issachar Reward	Chrysoprase Zebulun Tolerance	Hyacinth Joseph Trust	Amethyst Ben Truth	Jasper Judah Courage	Sapphire Reuben Faith	Chalcedony Gad Happiness
Sardonyx Naphtali Wrestlings understand	Sardius Manasseh Forgive	Chrysolite Simeon Hear	Beryl Levi Adherence	Topaz Issachar Reward	Chrysoprase Zebulun Tolerance	Hyacinth Joseph Trust	Amethyst Ben Truth	Jasper Judah Courage	Sapphire Reuben Faith	Chalcedony Gad Happiness	Emerald Asher Peace
Sardius Manasseh Forgive	Chrysolite Simeon Hear	Beryl Levi Adherence	Topaz Issachar Reward	Chrysoprase Zebulun Tolerance	Hyacinth Joseph Trust	Amethyst Ben Truth	Jasper Judah Courage	Sapphire Reuben Faith	Chalcedony Gad Happiness	Emerald Asher Peace	Sardonyx Naphtali Wrestlings understand
Chrysolite Simeon Hear	Beryl Levi Adherence	Topaz Issachar Reward	Chrysoprase Zebulun Tolerance	Hyacinth Joseph Trust	Amethyst Ben Truth	Jasper Judah Courage	Sapphire Reuben Faith	Chalcedony Gad Happiness	Emerald Asher Peace	Sardonyx Naphtali Wrestlings understand	Sardius Manasseh Forgive
Beryl Levi Adherence	Topaz Issachar Reward	Chrysoprase Zebulun Tolerance	Hyacinth Joseph Trust	Amethyst Ben Truth	Jasper Judah Courage	Sapphire Reuben Faith	Chalcedony Gad Happiness	Emerald Asher Peace	Sardonyx Naphtali Wrestlings understand	Sardius Manasseh Forgive	Chrysolite Simeon Hear
Topaz Issachar Reward	Chrysoprase Zebulun Tolerance	Hyacinth Joseph Trust	Amethyst Ben Truth	Jasper Judah Courage	Sapphire Reuben Faith	Chalcedony Gad Happiness	Emerald Asher Peace	Sardonyx Naphtali Wrestlings to understand	Sardius Manasseh Forgive	Chrysolite Simeon Hear	Beryl Levi Adherence
Chrysoprase Zebulun Tolerance	Hyacinth Joseph Trust	Amethyst Ben Truth	Jasper Judah Courage	Sapphire Reuben Faith	Chalcedony Gad Happiness	Emerald Asher Peace	Sardonyx Naphtali Wrestlings to understand	Sardius Manasseh Forgive	Chrysolite Simeon Hear	Beryl Levi Adherence	Topaz Issachar Reward
Hyacinth Joseph Trust	Amethyst Ben Truth	Jasper Judah Courage	Sapphire Reuben Faith	Chalcedony Gad Happiness	Emerald Asher Peace	Sardonyx Naphtali Wrestlings to understand	Sardius Manasseh Forgive	Chrysolite Simeon Hear	Beryl Levi Adherence	Topaz Issachar Reward	Chrysoprase Zebulun Tolerance
Amethyst Ben Truth	Jasper Judah Courage	Sapphire Reuben Faith	Chalcedony Gad Happiness	Emerald Asher Peace	Sardonyx Naphtali Wrestlings to understand	Sardius Manasseh Forgive	Chrysolite Simeon Hear	Beryl Levi Adherence	Topaz Issachar Reward	Chrysoprase Zebulun Tolerance	Hyacinth Joseph Trust

144,000 positive thoughts and actions of how to make Love whole in the whole spirit of Love.

Love with faith for discernment of righteousness for consciousness for friendship and unity for peace and security with repentance and forgiveness with grace for a restoration of the whole spirit of Love and a healing for *all nations.*

Faith to seek true happiness by turning away from sin to seek Love made whole thorough integrity to God's Love which is always positive and rewards loyalty with His spirit made whole in us. So be Love.

The mindset for salvation and redemption of the whole spirit of Love for Peace, Love and Joy to prevail for happiness for *All Nations,*

Amen. Ameen. Shalom, Namaste.

****

Contents

****

****

****

****

Parousia

Love's Light

****

How does The Light get in?

The Light sneaks in loudly,

quietly waiting, to be observed.

****

Bridge Ends

Bridgend, Pen-y-Bont
a tale of two bridges
bridging the gap
like the corpus callosum
bridges two halves;
hemispheres joined
making whole, making One
bridging Heaven and Earth
flesh and spirit
becoming One, becoming whole
0
two halves joined
bridged by the corpus callosum
like Jesus Christ bridges the gap
between man and God
between man and Love
Corpus Christi
the end of the arc of the bridge
is Golden.

****

Turquoise Love in Venice

Greeted by Atlas and church's galore
glorious in holy dedication
glorious in Turquoise Love
speaking glory to God
in the highest
in the domes
in the monasteries
the monuments.

Turquoise waters with
gondolas in reality,
not a painting.

The scent of sea weed
a taste of red wine and O lives
salt and fresh waters
flow freely.

****

Andréa's Gondola Ride

Two horses and an angel guide us perfectly
quiet sounds of water trickles as cool air
kisses my face with salty scents.

'Gondolas are eighth century wedding carriages
with no traffic or parking problems.
We have palaces galore;
The Doge's Palace the prime,
Contino's Ponte dei Sospiri;
The Bridge of Sighs crosses Rio di Palazzo.

Our Grand Canal is wider than it is deep
and forms a reverse S with
vaporettos as our water buses.

The Venice Lagoon
one hundred and eighteen islands
each with a church and palace
four hundred foot bridges
one hundred and seventy canals mingle and
merge with the Adriatic Sea
rich with fish, crabs, octopodes and oysters.

Gondoliers - we are like London taxi drivers
the knowledge learned, languages practiced
and no need for a gym.'

As we return
our Gondola horse rears on a wave
our angel ascends and
the sun sets beside St Marks Square.

Graci Andréa.

****

Il Paradiso (Fresco by Jacopo Tintoretto in the Doge's Palace, Venice)

Turquoise waters
glassy smooth in afternoon sun

Crystal foundations of freedom
sparkling in the dawn of the Son

Justice through Christ, through Christ's
justice, faith married with Positive Love

Paradise the vision, painted into words
in the Doge's Palace;

The Golden Staircase
exquisite extravaganzas of witnessing

Pictures painting thousands of words
penned over two thousand years ago

The virtues - the only way to paradise
Il Paradiso; peace for Heaven on Earth.

****

Sea Day to Dubrovnik

Sailing on a Sunday
sailing on The Son Day
a sunny day
lighted by the sun
lighted by The Son
a day of rest and recreation
The Sabbath Day, a sunny day, a Sunday
The Son's Day.

Old walled city of rock and light
sweet with sage, mint and magnolia
a Holy City
time too short, too much to see
Franciscan and Dominican monasteries;

Cloisters of heavenly jewels
gardens with trumpet flowers and
an apothecary with Crème de Rose.

****

Kotor Bay Spurs

Nature reigns these skylines and
cold winds greet us to a grey pre dawn.

Glacial spurs interlock where dwellings
with boats nestle elegantly at water's side.

A church bell rings and the scent
is mountain fresh woody earth.

Silence is broken only by the wind on my face.

It is dawn; 7am, and the bell rings again
and again, joined by another and another

Bells tolling with the reverence of Venice
though not waters of Turquoise Love but

Black Emerald lakes, deep, still, reflective.

Oceana drops her anchor and the sound
echoes vibrations like a quake.

A cockerel crows as another bell tolls
and I hear the sound of laughter.

****

Kotor Walls

I climb one step at a time
resting when I need
pairs of golden butterflies escort me
and Red Admirals swoop,
wafting close, reassuringly close.

Soft blue and yellow flowers grace the cliff's edge
and light pink cyclamen nestle under trees.

I climb one step at a time
at the halfway point, a
'church of good health' beckons

Cool cream chalked ceiling shines golden stars
and white roses grace the crystal alter as
ruby red clothes dress the windows.

I climb one step at a time
determinedly, one step at a time
grateful for the man selling water
grateful it was not the height of summer
grateful,

I climb one step at a time
at the summit an artist sells his visions
I share mine and I submit to a selfie.

****

Corfu Dawn

Sun rises behind mountains silhouetted on a golden canvas

a fine cross is silhouetted on the church on the headland
embracing the dawn, embracing the light

a dawn, different to yesterday, the dawning of a new light
for a new dawn of the Son's Light.

Corfu Town, home of the Corinthians
1st Corinthians 13, famous at many weddings

'and if I have the gifts of prophesying and am acquainted with all the sacred secrets and all knowledge, and if I have faith so as to transplant mountains, but do not have love, I am nothing.'

Love is always positive as a quantum cross
as a positive electron repels the negative
keeping energy pure and dynamic.

Greece, generosity in agape love
exquisite beauty in the bright white light rising.

I am comforted by the sound of bells again
and an aeroplane roars, defying gravity
as it rises into a sky blue sky.

I smell sunshine and feel warmth in my heart of
The Sons' shine.

****

Messina Straights

This morning I heard bells peeling
I saw a single dolphin leap, enjoying our wake

I wanted to see the pod and I wondered
where they might be

In the clouds I saw a dove like an angel and
horses gathering power

Prayers were said in morning service with grace and gratitude
and somehow I know I am where I am meant to be.

Civitavecchia

A day uncertain Rome or Civitavecchia?

Rome too daunting with crowds and expense.

Civitavecchia; Church of St Francis and the sea beckon
waters lighted like angels dancing delicately on water

We float in shallow water and
swim from a peace ship made from drift wood.

****

Breakfast in Napoli

Sun rises behind Vesuvius
a flock of 'wee' clouds float in from Sorrento
and nestle between two peaks

Two horses guard port
stamping on the serpent, stamping out the serpent
keeping pure

Cargo ships float by
and I taste grapefruit and prunes
fresh like dew.

****

San Martino Monastery, Naples

Blue light as a cross says 'here', 'here'

A moment eternal in the
'peace of God that excels all thought'

Blue Light as a cross says 'here,

'Here'

I looked around, only me, but I am not ready,
this is not Santa Engrácia.

Twelve crystal chambers at The Crystal Alter
prepared, waiting;
The painting; Christ in the Tomb, pre resurrection?
His consciousness realised is crystal clear, did they know?

Blue Light as a cross says 'Here' 'Here'

'Here'

Frozen, I capture the moment for proof of my sanity
Frozen, trembling I knew I would 'surely die' if I failed.

Blue Light as a cross demands; *'Here' 'Now'*
my heart palpates frantically, but I obey willingly.

After some time I find Pauline,
we share bread and red wine and Olives then descend
the pilgrims steps. We arrive at the fish market,
Octopi held captive still breathe, I see their air bubbles in water,
Octopodes have three hearts, they must be able to feel,
perhaps more than us?

Dome lit, we set sail as the sun sets behind Ischia
and I capture a bird soaring in red skies.

****

Cadiz Dawn

Pre dawn,
stormy darkness with bright lights:
an intermittent crescent moon
the cathedral
the light house
lightening strikes
and moving bright neon words protest:

Opressión
Desigualdad
Ignorancia
Injusticia
Absolutismos
Sumisión

I think I understand their meaning

(Oppression, inequality, ignorance, injustice, absolutism, submission.)

****

Cadiz 'Coast of Light'

City of light and silver waters
sea thunders on rocks
elements ghost the air
sea salts season
waves cresting like
Andalucían stallions rearing
dancing
manes flowing, flying

Power perfectly harnessed
surfers conquering
breakwaters misting and
silver light bathes my skin.

Elements

Lanzarote Igneous Mountains

Molten
lava molded
fodder flowing forth from
an eternal scarlet ocean, eruptions
of heat ignite a metamorphism of elements
creating crystallised gems of and for Love.

****

Dust to Dust

We are made of stardust
elements combined, minerals
communicating, antagonising
responding, relaxing, replenishing

Fuels made from the stars
supernovas in us
stellar explosions making new
minerals, crystals, salts, elements
mined from His earth and His heavens.

Moon moves waters
making us turbulent seas of molecules
crystallising life
in this desert storm of stardust.

****

****

La Palma Mammary Mountain

*

Mammary
of a mountain
holds memory in magma
elements hot, molten in subterranean
lakes of liquid fire, pressure rising like blood
gaining momentum, waiting to erupt waiting to rupture
cancers to create and breast feed The Promised New World.

****

Molten Molecules of Creation

Iron molecules molten; spinning like a wheel of fortune for us here on a microsphere in this macro galaxy of milky stars showing their ways on cloudless nights

elements bursting red giants; firework supernovas exploding into macro lights into micro lights, white dwarfs imploding black holes:

density, decay, destruction 'til death: recycling regenerating, renewing 'til life; resurrecting;

atoms of hydrogen becoming helium floating, flaring, raring free to bring the light to unite and warm humanity;

atoms of hydrogen, bonding oxygen for water - for us to grow like flowers able to blossom trees able to fruit birds singing;

Iron molecules molten; spinning like a wheel of fortune inside us; haemoglobin in our hearts, our core, our blood: the life force within; pumping, beating oxygenating our micro cells with macro elements periodically fuelling our souls for some hazy, lazy summer daze of love...

dust to dust; macro to micro to macro to micro; hydrogen to helium to hydro carbons

lead can lead to gold with atoms and elements salsa dancing life.

****

A New Heaven: New Jerusalem

Revelation 21

Everything real is invisible;
gifts of jasper transformed from pearls
emeralds made from sapphires squared
attaining to amethysts shining like
diamonds dancing delicately on water
chalcedony waltzing with topaz
sardonyx serenading sardius
turquoise passions speaking Love
Love being made whole like and olivine
fulfilling complete
like a mine of treasures with no dragon
no pirates or opposition
just understanding with reason
chrysolite gold molten into an emerald river
flowing to a chrysoprase sea.

****

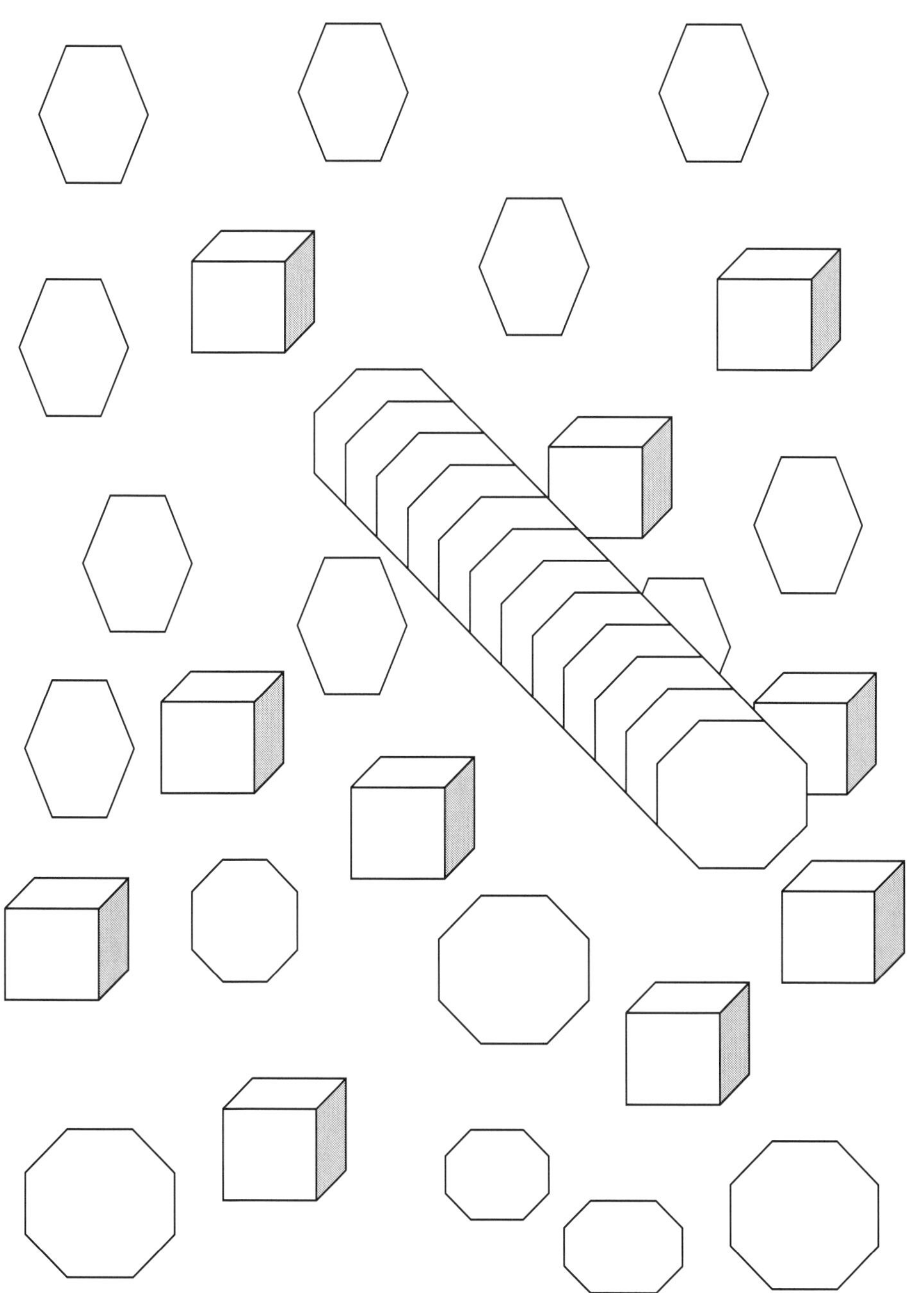

****

God's Healing Love

(My interpretation from the gemstones and tribes of Israel cited in The Book of Revelation as reasoned in *Healing Poems for Positive Love, Book of Life*, and yet to be published, *Little Gems for Healing Love,* and the concepts delivered in all my poetry).

Love has courage to seek fulfillment of happiness by turning away
from sin with courage as jasper and rubies like Judah
and faith as blue as Reuben sapphires
happiness colourful as Gad and chalcedony
with the peace of Asher and emeralds
wrestlings of good and bad, haram and halal, Naphtali, sardonyx
choices for forgiveness as Manasseh, sardius
(perhaps also forgiveness of the exiled firstborn son Ishmael)
Listening, hearing as Simeon - golden chrysolite
adhering as Levi, beryl, emeralds,
Love with peace for the endorphin reward of topaz, Issachar
With the tolerance of chrysoprase, Zebulun
trust of Joseph, blue Hyacinth sapphires for faith
truth through grieving pain, mourning as Ben
for attaining the pure truth and healing
for the trust, security and peace of
amethyst Love.
'know the truth and the truth will set you free' John 8:32

****

The Therapeutic Process for Healing Love.

Courage;* to seek **happiness* and fulfillment of Love; *Courage;* to repent and turn away from sin withFaith;* in happiness and fulfillment for **peace*. **Wrestlings;* with understandings - haram/ halal, good/bad right/wrong/healthy for conscious understanding to **forgive, to *Hear*; actively **listen*, empathise, understand and **adhere* too, be loyal too **Reward*; endorphin reward of Love 'just as in the twinkling of an eye' - a nervous system response with
**Tolerance*; patience and **trust* in faith and love for peace via
**Truth*; 'only truth can set us free' via our conscience; free from our own pains which are individual and all pain is caused by sin of some type. Truth is God's Love made whole in Oneness with self and others and God. God is Love, God causes to become, Love made whole in us, we are Love - Oneness with God and there is only One, only One Love made whole worthy of honour.

Jasper Judah Courage	Sapphire Reuben Faith	Chalcedony Gad Happiness	Emerald Asher Peace	Sardonyx Naphtali Wrestlings understand	Sardius Manasseh Forgive	Chrysolite Simeon Hear	Beryl Levi Adherence	Topaz Issachar Reward	Chrysoprase Zebulun Tolerance	Hyacinth Joseph Trust	Amethyst Ben Truth
Sapphire Reuben Faith	Chalcedony Gad Happiness	Emerald Asher Peace	Sardonyx Naphtali Wrestlings understand	Sardius Manasseh Forgive	Chrysolite Simeon Hear	Beryl Levi Adherence	Topaz Issachar Reward	Chrysoprase Zebulun Tolerance	Hyacinth Joseph Trust	Amethyst Ben Truth	Jasper Judah Courage
Chalcedony Gad Happiness	Emerald Asher Peace	Sardonyx Naphtali Wrestlings understand	Sardius Manasseh Forgive	Chrysolite Simeon Hear	Beryl Levi Adherence	Topaz Issachar Reward	Chrysoprase Zebulun Tolerance	Hyacinth Joseph Trust	Amethyst Ben Truth	Jasper Judah Courage	Sapphire Reuben Faith
Emerald Asher Peace	Sardonyx Naphtali Wrestlings understand	Sardius Manasseh Forgive	Chrysolite Simeon Hear	Beryl Levi Adherence	Topaz Issachar Reward	Chrysoprase Zebulun Tolerance	Hyacinth Joseph Trust	Amethyst Ben Truth	Jasper Judah Courage	Sapphire Reuben Faith	Chalcedony Gad Happiness
Sardonyx Naphtali Wrestlings understand	Sardius Manasseh Forgive	Chrysolite Simeon Hear	Beryl Levi Adherence	Topaz Issachar Reward	Chrysoprase Zebulun Tolerance	Hyacinth Joseph Trust	Amethyst Ben Truth	Jasper Judah Courage	Sapphire Reuben Faith	Chalcedony Gad Happiness	Emerald Asher Peace
Sardius Manasseh Forgive	Chrysolite Simeon Hear	Beryl Levi Adherence	Topaz Issachar Reward	Chrysoprase Zebulun Tolerance	Hyacinth Joseph Trust	Amethyst Ben Truth	Jasper Judah Courage	Sapphire Reuben Faith	Chalcedony Gad Happiness	Emerald Asher Peace	Sardonyx Naphtali Wrestlings understand
Chrysolite Simeon Hear	Beryl Levi Adherence	Topaz Issachar Reward	Chrysoprase Zebulun Tolerance	Hyacinth Joseph Trust	Amethyst Ben Truth	Jasper Judah Courage	Sapphire Reuben Faith	Chalcedony Gad Happiness	Emerald Asher Peace	Sardonyx Naphtali Wrestlings understand	Sardius Manasseh Forgive
Beryl Levi Adherence	Topaz Issachar Reward	Chrysoprase Zebulun Tolerance	Hyacinth Joseph Trust	Amethyst Ben Truth	Jasper Judah Courage	Sapphire Reuben Faith	Chalcedony Gad Happiness	Emerald Asher Peace	Sardonyx Naphtali Wrestlings understand	Sardius Manasseh Forgive	Chrysolite Simeon Hear
Topaz Issachar Reward	Chrysoprase Zebulun Tolerance	Hyacinth Joseph Trust	Amethyst Ben Truth	Jasper Judah Courage	Sapphire Reuben Faith	Chalcedony Gad Happiness	Emerald Asher Peace	Sardonyx Naphtali Wrestlings to understand	Sardius Manasseh Forgive	Chrysolite Simeon Hear	Beryl Levi Adherence
Chrysoprase Zebulun Tolerance	Hyacinth Joseph Trust	Amethyst Ben Truth	Jasper Judah Courage	Sapphire Reuben Faith	Chalcedony Gad Happiness	Emerald Asher Peace	Sardonyx Naphtali Wrestlings to understand	Sardius Manasseh Forgive	Chrysolite Simeon Hear	Beryl Levi Adherence	Topaz Issachar Reward
Hyacinth Joseph Trust	Amethyst Ben Truth	Jasper Judah Courage	Sapphire Reuben Faith	Chalcedony Gad Happiness	Emerald Asher Peace	Sardonyx Naphtali Wrestlings to understand	Sardius Manasseh Forgive	Chrysolite Simeon Hear	Beryl Levi Adherence	Topaz Issachar Reward	Chrysoprase Zebulun Tolerance
Amethyst Ben Truth	Jasper Judah Courage	Sapphire Reuben Faith	Chalcedony Gad Happiness	Emerald Asher Peace	Sardonyx Naphtali Wrestlings to understand	Sardius Manasseh Forgive	Chrysolite Simeon Hear	Beryl Levi Adherence	Topaz Issachar Reward	Chrysoprase Zebulun Tolerance	Hyacinth Joseph Trust

****

I Am: The One: Love

(Exodus 3;14 ' I AM WHAT I AM' : ' I SHALL PROVE TO BE WHAT I SHALL PROVE TO BE;' Love Proven.)

'I AM WHAT I AM'
The One: One Love
Oneness in only the I
resonating wholeness in Love
all chakras firing.

Am I One?
or are my parts f r a g m e n t e d
unreachable without Oneness
when I am not whole, when I am not One
but broken into a million smithereens
shattered like a windscreen still in one piece
searching for the Oneness
Wholeness in 'The I Am'
Oneness in wholeness in Love
The One; The I; The I AM
1 Love.

Process of self actualization via reason and truth.
Concept of Sir Muhammad Iqbal's Khudi – selfhood and
Samuel Taylor Coleridge's self actualization and renewal of self through imagination and reason.
The therapeutic process for healing Love to become whole.

****

A Philosophical Pythagoras Poem for Creating Healing Love and Light

Everything and nothing, an eve of no and thing, particles of nothingness
like black is every colour and at the same time an absence of colour
dark and dense, a vacuum, opposite to light
like light emits a source of no vacuum but a flow like a river of energy giving and making a river of Love
hydrogen and oxygen, helium from above, somewhere in the heavens that are there
light removed from the dark black, separated from the chaos creating order, creating two, opposition that lives in us too as positive and negative, lightness and dark, lightness and heaviness that needs
a spark of sparkling stars like sparklers sparkling on an autumn night
magnesium explosions like Coq10 in our hearts
that we can only see with an absence of day in the dark night
becoming the day through dawn
through mellow yellows and orange pinks, a rising fireball that makes me think
there must be something, something that makes us see
something from this chemistry in this mystery of physics and geometry giving us a matrix for life, something in this chaotic soup of everything and no thing
heaviness and light and darkness and light and night and day and wrong and right and dim and bright light stars guiding to gold and myrrh and frankincense;

Frank in sense: senses coming together like a village common for common good for the community to commune,
senses coming together making six and seven rays of input making whole, whole and holes like no and every thing
like string strung strong theories theorising everything
when some things are beyond theories, beyond measure like pleasing pleasures that are so beyond measure except by the feeling the feeling of being alive;

****

of cells tingling, vibrations communicating, connecting, making, building creating light and light energy of gifting abundance and dark and dark energy of density and
vacuums of giving or taking;
like mathematics,
adding up to profit or loss, multiplying what you give,
attracting more of every thing or no thing;

Health and wealth or ills and pills creating the windowsills we sit and view our life from
the rectangular, arched or round window,
a glass half full or empty
packed full of crystals and grains of sand and just when you think it can contain no more, it can be filled with water
and add some heat and you can make clouds
and add some light and you can make a rainbow that you can see;

Who says we can't see the light?

Because light has colour, rays ordered and separated into frequencies of vibration
resonance, colours making sound that we can hear,
filling voids with healing light
frequencies making sound, making whole, harmonising Love.

Love capturing crystal rainbows for healing life
rain bowing, light arching light to earth
creating visions of hope, colours that we can see
with an absence of dark,
with an absence of no and everything.

****

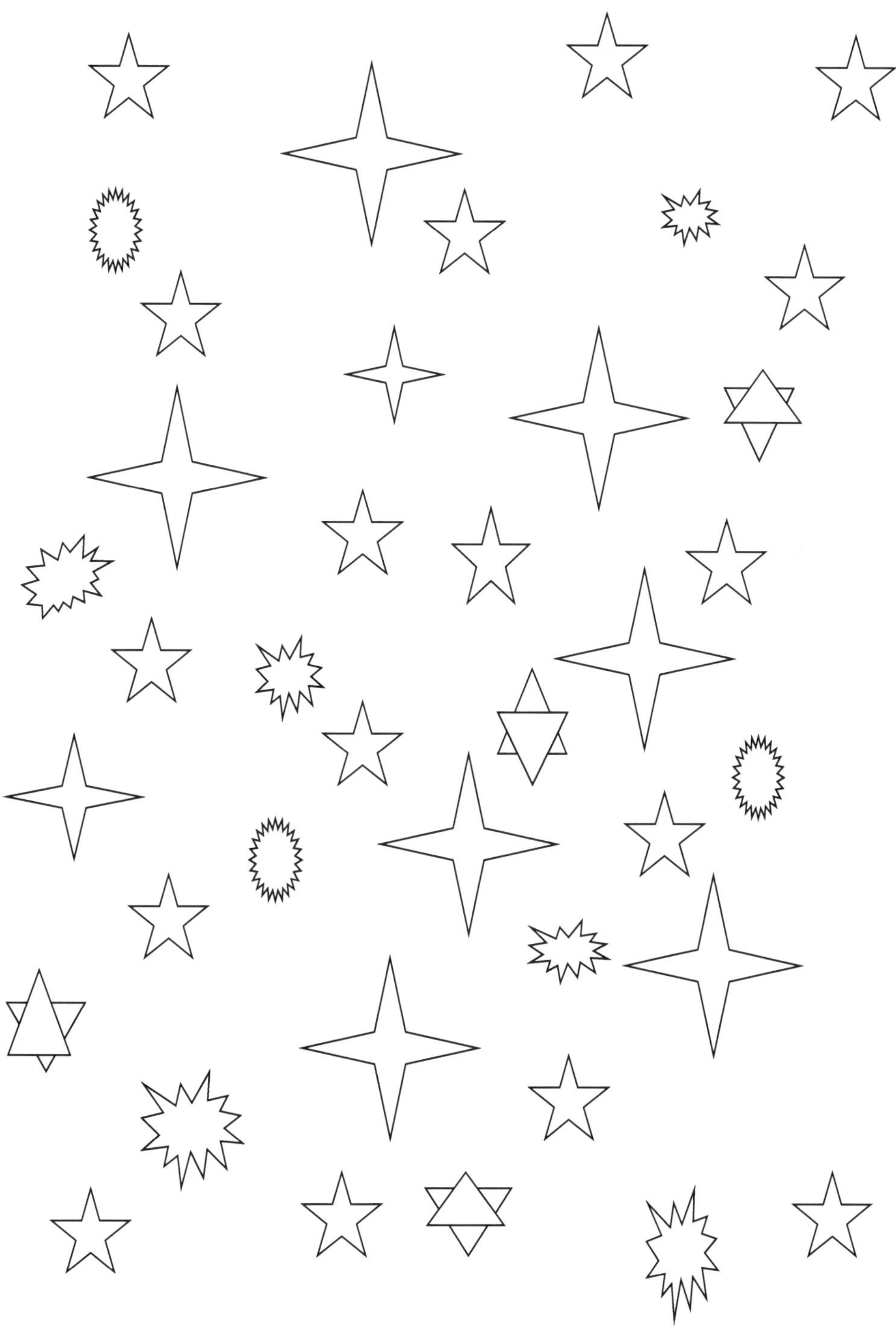

****

Reasoning Love

Love is the reason. The reason we live, the reason we survive
the reason we use to reason because only Love is reasonable.

Love is why. Love is why we know right from wrong
wrong from right, haram from halal; Love is why we know.

We know. We know what is wrong and we know what is right.
We know because we feel.

We feel good or not good. Good or bad, strong or weak
happy or sad, hope or despair; confusion.

We know what we feel.

We feel positive or negative, hope or faith or fear.
Positive, faithful, happy on course or negative, fearful and frightened,

Stressed: A Mess: Messed up.

No Love in stress and no Love in fear, because stress is not Love,
Anxiety is not Love, betrayal is not Love. Love is not a cortisol.

Love is reasonable; it will reason the wrongs with itself,
Love will ask why?

Who, where, what, when? Who Doctor? Doctor who, why?
Love is the Doctor making conscious.

Conscious of the hurt, the pain the injustice, the loss of peace, the loss of Love, Love is the Doctor making conscious.

Consciousness for confiding, making conscious the wrong to put right for consciousness
self conscious for understanding confidence in Love and self actualisation;

****

Reasoning; understanding the reason to be able to heal by prescribing Love for Love for Love to become Love to become whole Love in a Positive spirit

Spirits combined and doubled as Ephraim, Jerusalem becoming whole, whole as One Love;

One being who is whole, fulfilled with spirit of joy enthused with patience, kindness, peace, Love, joy, faith;

Faith in Love, faith with Love, faith that Love will become for wholeness in us that is Love for sharing,

Faith that Love will become whole and One

No fragments detached or broken by short changing Love with adrenalin, Love is not a cortisol.

Love is the beginning , the middle and the end,
The Alpha and Omega

Love is the end point, the endorphin, Love is The Point
otherwise there is no point, no reason;

Love is the reason. Love is the only reason, the endpoint of Love;

'To be or not to be' Love, that *is* the question

Love *is* the reason, the reason *is* Love.

****

Madeira: Island of Heavenly Flowers

I smell the scent of peace
lilies waft fragrances like jasmine and rose
stabilised with frankincense and myrrh
laden with sandalwood
Heaven on Earth.

****

Lisbon Approach

Good morning
sunrise is a relief after a night like Jonah
helicopter rescue successful
fear hits me, claustrophobia raging.

Train rhythm syncopates
over the hum of our engines
two planes circle and water
breaks over submerged submarine.

Sun rises over suspension bridge as
terracotta roofs greet the dawn
I see Him by the bridge
Christ the King, arms open wide

waiting to embrace...

Pilots come to greet us
seagulls join to ride the thermals
and passengers capture moments;
columns, statues, football stadium

Black taxis with blue green roofs
red and yellow tour buses, builders busy
in the distance Jerónimos Monastery sits above
the dome of Panteao National, Church of Santa Engrácia

beckoning for 'work that takes a long time to complete'.

****

Parousia

I think when He comes again the sky will turn soft pink with a
golden haze and wild magenta dashes
there will be warmth in your heart, my heart and everyone's
hearts will beat as one with Love.

When He comes again will we be ready;
will we have prepared our bodies ;
can we reside in His Love without betrayals, greed and war;
Can Love reside with fear?

When He comes again are we ready to embrace Him?
I am ready to soar beyond the moon and stars
perch on Jupiter's moons, float the rings of Saturn
and drop to Earth in a flash;

Sapphire blue planet Earth, water we are all made up of
hydrogen and oxygen, elements we share
molecular patterns harmonising, uniting life.

When the sun shines water evaporates into clouds
and 'in every cloud there is a rainbow'
rainbows join you and me with the sky and sea
can you see them?

Auras emitting colours, waters reflecting
frequencies of Loves' Light of Love:
With His Love can all be rainbows?
Can all be Light?

****

Light Beings: $E = MC^2$ (Albert Einstein's formula applied to our cells)

We are light beings lighted with Love
when finding our souls' passions in every delight
we are light beings sent from heaven above.

Finding our hearts' wings when white like doves
speaking our truths expelling the darkness of night
we are light beings when lighted with Love.

Saying our truths to speak of Heaven's Love
is like the sun shining, sons shining new Light
we are light beings sent from heaven above.

We are light beings ignited by Love
lighting us with light thoughts that are bright
we are light beings when lighted with Love.

Physical mass times the speed of Love
is physical mass times the speed of Light
we *can* be light beings from heaven above.

Physical mass times the speed of Love
resonates Love's energy for attaining to Light
we are light beings when lighted with Love
we are light beings sent from heaven above.

****

Chakras and Saints

Colours bright as an inquisitive child
visions swirling, Light bridging worlds

Colours dimmed with pain
grey with cancer, dark and black with death

Colours bright as a playful child
Light as a rainbow across a waterfall

Colours oiled like paintings
Love forming golden halos.

****

'I think therefore I am' René Descartes

Religions are a way of thinking
we are what we think

'I think therefore I am'
if we do not think what are we?

I think a holiday is a Holy Day, a whole day
free from enslavement
for cultivating the whole spirit of joy

I think what are we without Love
without positivity?

Do we 'positively die'?
and if so
then what do we become?

****

Scaffolding

Supporting the matrix
the horizontal negative crossed with the vertical
positively clamped in place,
nuts bolted; screwed together
forming 144,000 squares squared making
288,000 triangles of

Hope

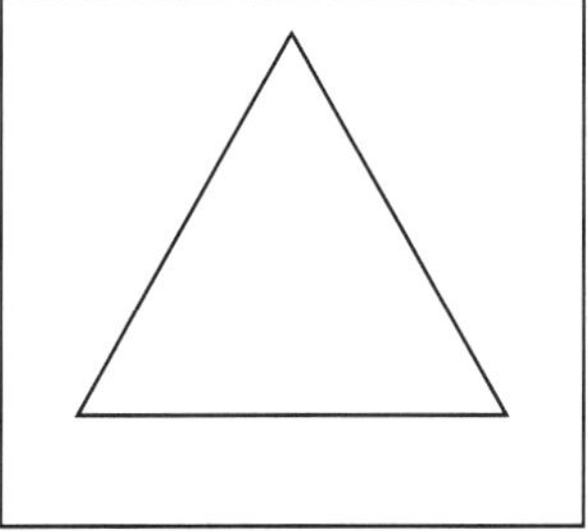

Love Faith

The only foundations needed for building
The New Paradise for renewing Eden:
Heaven on Earth
where happiness can Positively dwell.

****

****

Adam, Eve and St Agnes (will learn war no more) Isaiah 2:4

Oh! what if St Agnes had been in the Garden of Eden
on that fateful day, could we be living in paradise now?
Would we be living in paradise now?
Perhaps, just, maybe...

Could we be positively living with no hurts or pain?
Just love and kindness
No jealousy, no crime, no sickness, no shame

No death of Love, no death of the Positive Spirit, no death of joy
No wars - just 'wonderful counsel': no wars - just 'Princely peace'
No wars - an 'eternal parent guiding'

What is the point of fighting? All for the same thing anyway;
that elusive prize of Positive Life; peace and love for our loved ones

'Do beat your swords into plowshares and your spears into pruning shears' as it is written (Isaiah)

Go grow your own paradise and your own food
grow your own herbs and your own flowers,
learn grace for self control, autonomy and self worth,
heal and grow in Positive Spirit

Love each other as yourself, Love your neighbour and be kind
give love freely as Love takes time.

Strong, yet fragile; Sacred

One betrayal will burst Love's bubble.
We become negative and fearful; not able to trust
so never betray and we can Positively Live now.

Oh St Agnes, where were you that fateful day
when mankind Positively Died?

****

Distilling Love

To remove the taste of Judas

take Bach flower remedy of crab apple
add sulphur

wash with apple cider vinegar and
bathe in Bach's Toccata and Fugue

waft with Frankincense and bathe with Myrrh

blend oil of Rose with essence of Jasmine
shake a little and infuse for Sophia

distil 'til clear   like a perfumed memory
of first love's kiss on a summer's eve.

****

To be or not be Love

It is funny how I thought it would be easy
I thought it would be easy;
I really thought it would be easy

I thought *you* would be delighted with the data analysis
the observations observed and the conclusions concluded are
conclusive,

They were quite simple really; the principles were not new,
they are not new, but I knew,
I could see that the science backed up the principles: –

It is fantastically obvious and obviously fantastic –
how could it not be? How could it not be? How can it not be?
It could not, not be, it had to be, it has to be, it will be...

I will tell you a little secret; it has to be,
it is the promise for life you see; What? You may well ask;

'To be or not to be' is the question - but it is so much more than a
question, to be is the answer to everything:

When we are not being true, we are being something else,
something we are not meant to be,
something we are not, therefore a lie;

A lie is not our truth and is not Love, Not Love, Not Love.

Not Love is not being Love. Not Love is not being. Not Love is not
being Love; which is not Love.

You see it is Love we are meant to be and Love needs no rules to be,
except Love…

Love rules Love and causes Love to become;

****

Love is never hurtful or unkind. Love needs to be and Love has to be, it is the only way to be,

But hey - it is not easy in a world full of vices wanting to
entices us away from Love, away from Love, away from Love.

How can it be that you and me fall short, are short changed
the dream?
The dream of Love becoming One; Love becoming whole
Love?

Well only by not being Love and allowing not Love to be
which is not heavenly and it is not being Love in being;

It is not being Love; it is not being Love which is not being;

This is how we be, by being Love, by being Love enthused to make us optimistic positive beings with hope of Love,

Faith in Love, certainty in Love, for Love to be enthused beings,
human beings, loving beings, happy beings

and so it goes on ad infinitum, to infinity and beyond:
Eternal; So be Love;

Love in being: To be is the only answer to Love
to infuse Love to enthuse Love for Love to be enthused,
infused into us to be Love.

So Be It. Amen, Ameen. Shalom, Namaste.

****

****

Artificial Intelligence

Slipped in softly, secretly behind the scenes where
idleness meets idolatry: idolatry fuels idleness
mimicking like two year olds in nursery
autonomy yet to learn, autonomy sidelined automatically
order dictated, freedom thwarted
mothers enslaved to automated traffic lights
in automobiles on auto drive
speeding for school 'pick up'
men 'picking up' more mothers to be
passions thwarted, love diverted
released as an archer's bow
in the name of safety
touch an abuse, mis-touch the abuse
no touch an abuse
ignorance the ignorer
isolation the pinnacle
independence the poster
loneliness the product
automated
intelligence forgotten
sold out; artificial
no art in artificial
artificial intelligence
can only be a contradiction
of ITself.

****

Games of Hunger

Careless power games with hungry games of power. That internal
asking question deep
inside their core; aching, screaming, crying, for something to
alkalize the acid that burns
the hole eroding the essence of life.

'Food glorious food.' The right of every living being, to realise
the potential of Hippocrates words:
'Let food be thy medicine and medicine be thy food' for healing
and sustaining life;
switching on the bright lights of the soul; Light energy for the life
force within.

'Though not by bread alone' - there is darkness in only white bread;
when empty food
poisons the soul being fatally controlled by invisible powers of
wanton desires that be fat
cats who know no care, nor grace
reapers, rapers, takers

Remember Charles Dickens' Oliver Twist and Nancy who asked not
only for more but
'Where is Love?' Where is The Love that cares for the orphaned
child,
the broken child of the battered wife of the wayward husband?
Where is The Love that fills
the black acid hole of hunger with nutritious food, the Love that fills
loneliness with
friendship and makes us whole in the spirit of peaceful joy?
Where is The Love from the words that feed us all medicinal
nourishing food?
The Word(s) that do not allow hunger.

Apocalyptic Poem (Revelation 6: famine, pestilence, war)

The red, black and pale horse ride with thunder...
Thunderous clouds of hail and snow
Bringing cold wherever they go
Reaching to lands far and wide
Going to affect many new brides
Not what she had planned for her wedding day
Psychopathic games being played
Games of hunger, death and thrones
Ice reaching inside, inside to her bones
Reaching the marrow, harrowing thoughts
Causing divisions of all sorts
Dichotomies of the mind,
Tipping the scales away from man being kind
Tipping to fractions of slated grey
Slavery to states of being not gay
Slavery to hunger, thirst and no day
Slavery to making no hay
Slavery riding into the day
Galloping our freedoms away
Causing the blood to rage like the sea
Burning as an ember tree
Causing the charcoal to burn somewhere new
Making potash a chance to renew
Time to release the pure white horse
Jousting with the paler horse
Knocking him far off course
With a new form of discourse
The red horse cannot fail to stumble
Causing all the greed to crumble
Causing the black horse to turn his back
And turn around and head right back
Into the darkness, the density.
Time to bring out the new city of gold
That we have been waiting from times of old
Galloping white horses bringing the food
To avoid those negative moods
Making fields of darkness white like snow
Placing footprints, showing which way to go.

****

War

Explosions exploiting - men's balls and egos
Explosions exploiting - the land, air and sea foes
Conflicting thoughts - of thoughts, land and love
Conflicting thoughts - not from heaven above.

Conflict that blows off - heads, arms and legs
Conflict that stops men - sleeping in beds
Conflict that arises from stress and from fear
Conflict creating more than one tear.

Conflict of man - only hurts, maims and kills
Conflict of man - makes us all stressed on pills
Conflict of man - from seeking his thrills
Gives to the world - a skin full of chills.

Conflicts are only mans egos with issues;
Conflicts are best dealt with therapy and tissues.

****

Israel

Jerusalem in Israel, was once green and pleasant
But now only dust war, is the present
Dust of dark dirt, flesh, eyes and bones
Dust of dark history, hope, faith and homes.

Dust of blood bombs form the homeless
Dust of conflict from the faithless
Dust of Jacob's forgotten sons
Remembering only oil based sums.

Well these are sums that I do dwell
That 666 equals hell
Hell on earth to take the peace
With every single war, one piece.

One piece of peace is lost with each soul;
Surely it is positive to teach love as whole.

****

666 (Revelation 13)

Sin is anti Christ, anti whole; incomplete
falling short of Love made whole in mind,
in body, in spirit.

Falling short of the corpus callosum
Falling short of corpus Christi
not joining eternally in flows of infinite 8's;
888 in mind, in body, in spirit.

No positive crossovers for a positive life
with 144 thousand Positive thoughts made whole;
000 for creating Oneness in Love.

666 lacks completeness in Love made whole (8,0)
666 is the number of 'The Beast'
Flesh without spirit: Manmean, MeanMen or women
666 is fear in mind, body and self
cultivating fear for war and conflict everywhere.

****

Jerusalem

Oh green and pleasant land of the dove
What has happened to peace and love?
For Jerusalem that was being made here
Is now being turned into terror and fear.

Oh green and pleasant land do you hear?
That Jerusalem that was made here
Is peace that is meant to be
From living a good life, positively.

Positively living means not to die
From negativity, that is the lie
Lies from loves opposition called stress
It is stress that creates in us, such a mess.

Jerusalem; negative you are not meant to be;
But healing the lands with Positivity; +.

****

Hurricane Shahid (After You by Agha Shahid Ali)

It will be perfectly executed
when they find the rooms and rooms of charts
navigation routes routed to Our Fathers House

Treasures revealed;
the Holy Grail full, filled full
that no pirates or opposition can loot
and snow white truths will awaken dwarfs
into giant mines for growing Sapphire and
Turquoise Love; perhaps in Kashmir.

How many know these treasures
these truths that He says 'seek and ye shall find'.

'When will the doomsday be?' you Shahid ask
and you say you were 'put on hold'
and I Francess say
'the doomsday will be the day before the light returns'.

****

The End

The end is the start of the beginning of the word endorphin
the end of the quest for heart smiles in Love
mimicked by opium posing as opiates
killing pain knowing pleasure
addictive, seductive, seducing
ending enslavement to cortisols crying for an end
the end; the release of endorphins
the dopamine, the serotonin, the oxytocin , the anandamide
binding the blood in marriage with Love
which is always positive
the endorphin is the end
the end is the beginning of the word endorphin
His Love in our blood
The end is the beginning of freedom
The end is the beginning of The Promise.

****

~~~~~~~~~Water Levels of Consciousness~~~~~~~

The waters are damned.
There is no flow.
There are blocks.

Water does not like division and separation at different levels
there is a desire within, a calling to unite, a desire and calling
to be one, a desire and calling to river together to gather together
as one sea ~~~~~~
we are the sea; ~~~~~~~~~~ we are like water; ~~~~~~~~~~~~~
we must see that only in oneness are we level and whole~~~~~
see, the destiny of humanity is to be one sea~~~~~~~~~~~~~~
~~~~~~
~~~~~~
~~~~~~
~~~~~~
~~~~~~
~~~~~~
~~~~~~
~~~~~~
~~~~~~
~~~~~~
~~~~~~
~~~~~~
~~~~~~
~~~~~~
~~~~~~
~~~~~~
~~~~~~
~~~~~~
~~~~~~
~~~~~~
~~~~~~
~~~~~~
~~~~~~

****
~~~~~~

Watermark

Isn't it time to hit the middle road
stop weaving left and right
and just do what is right by all?

Time to stop meandering through stagnant failures
and water falling profits in one direction
stop locking the water and stop damming the flow.

Open up the reservoirs of wealth
melt the icebergs of fear
let abundance flow to the people

Make waves of contentment
tsunamis of opportunities
raise the tide mark for prosperity

Sift out the sewage
and let people surf to a
prosperous new world.

****

Peace One Day (Philippians 4:7)

How far away is peace one day?
One day then two makes life better for you...
and me...then, we can have three...then maybe four
for more to live and to Love in harmony.

With self and with others harmonious Love
for harmony with nature and peace from above.
The planets and moon mean peace very soon
so please do tune to 'the peace of Love that
excels all thought' and makes home for a dove.

Have faith that the good will conquer the evil
and that Love can conquer the fear
it is so very near and clear that when Love conquers all
man can walk tall.

With Love there's no fear, only things we hold dear
no need to conquer or blame one another
then we can be, a true community
with man united by the peace of Love
that is home for The Dove.

Yeh, Peace everyday is not far away.

****

Building Bridges: One Love

The ravines are deep and swirling
East and West merging new waters
emerging for rapture
fountains of peace to the world

Islam, imaan, dua; peace faith and worship of Love
of Oneness in us

No divisions, no sects,   no harm, no haram, just
Halal, Hallelujah for all
freedom through Love creating trust
causing Love to become One, One whole
Holy, the whole truth and nothing but the truth

Self actualisation
seeking the pain and loss with reason
Love is the reason

La ilaha illallah, YHWH, JHVH, Yashua, Brahman, Buddha
Ohmmmmmmmmmmmmmmmmmmmmmmmmmmmmmm

Is it not the meaning of the name which is truth?
Let us all become One,
Humane through One Love made whole in us
Love is always Positive.

(Inclusive of all positive belief systems not named, 'A Healing for *All nations*).

****

A Ghazal

If I lived in Kashmir would I wear a pharin in the depths of snowy winter
with a kangris? just as you do

And if you lived in Wales would you open an umbrella to shelter
from 'even the (horizontal) rain'? just as we do

If I had grown up with your mother tongue and name for God
I would speak the same language as you

And if I had grown up with your customs
would I have had to do?

If my church was a mosque
I would go to mosque like you do

If your mosque was a church
would you go to church? as I sometimes do

If in a Hindu or Bhuddist Temple
I would join om as they do

Ohmmmmmmmmmmmmmmmmmmmmmmmmmmmmmm

And when in school with philosophers
I will debate as they do

And if in the desert with my horse
I would pray there too

When eating lunch of spinach, rice and cheese
I will give thanks as it is right to do

Is freedom halal for you and hallelujah for me?
Seeking unity, peace and freedom is all we can do

And I Francess love to set free the divinity in we
just as all with love and hope do.

Kashmir Snow

Snow as stars
falling to be picked as flowers

New constellations blanketing
Ruby hearts and Sapphire smiles

Snow as flakes of heaven
landing full of promise.

Divinity

Imagination
imagine feeling well
imagine being well
imagine
imagine feeling full of energy
abundance of joy
vitality
smiling Love and faith
imagine
imagine beauty beyond humans
beauty in one hundred shades of green
one thousand golden sunflowers
ten thousand ruby roses
one million jasmine flowers
imagine the sweet scent
lingering
divine
imagine the divine
a sense of being alive
a divine state of being
Imagine being divine.

****

Life

Life is not about what religion
But about our faith in the good.

Life is not about what colour
but about our compassion and humanity.

Life is not about what gender
but about our thinking and reasoning abilities.

Life is not about sex
but about feelings, care and making love.

Life is not about anxiety, stress and fear
but about love, hope and trust.

Life is not about fighting, enmity and violence
but about peace, harmony, trust and faith.

Life is not about fear and negativity
but about being positive, loving and kind.

Life is wonderful if and only if
we cultivate Positive Love.

****

Ideal Ideas (for the Atheists and Agnostics)

Ideal ideas
salvaging souls
lost and suffering;

Ideal ideas
releasing pain
lifting weights
revealing;

Ideal ideas
knowing
ideal solutions
to make perfect
complete and whole.

Ideal ideas
from where?

****

Life Energy

Joy, laughter and a smile
lasting more than a little while

Aglow inside energises a glow outside
illuminating a rainbow aura with
golden positive light flowing like the river of life
cells firing madly, communicating rapidly
switching on the processes to life;

Pure and golden white light
like an angel in the night
have no fear, only Love and we can live
with the hope from above;

All pain released, processed and forgotten
forgiven and bonded by Love for union
and unity, peace, goodwill and grace.

Contentment and fulfillment with a happy smile
make this life *so* worthwhile.

****

Sonnet for a Loving God

If God had a healing method what would it be?
Would it be based on science and chemistry?
Chemistry not of the laboratory kind
But chemistry born in the blood out of mind.

How can mind do that you may ask?
And I may say this is a complex task
A complex task this may be
To attain to thoughts that are heavenly.

It seems to me we have lost the divine
Who gives us the power to love all the time
In whom does it make a difference to create
Let me assure you there is no mistake;

Only His Love teaches wholeness of mind
Only His Love teaches gentleness for Man to be kind.

****

Poppies

Floppy poppies floating in the sun
Are a source of joy for everyone
They should grow amongst the wheat we eat
And in small doses are a treat.

Like frankincense they conquer fear
But only if we respect them dear
They help remove the pain of man
But wont fulfil the challenge or plan.

You see it is up to us to grow
Like scarlet poppies in the snow
Fighting off the frost and cold with
Loves golden, reddened glow.

When we find that golden glow
Our own opiates we can grow.

****

Oceana

Oceana you have shown to me
The freedom found from roaming the seas
Ports with history beyond compare
Showing origins of life made beautiful and fair;

Fair in kindness; virtues that stealth
Creating justice, freedom and wealth
Wealth not of the monetary kind,
But wealth from love's joy, created in mind;

It is in our mind we create the faith
It is in our hearts we feel the faith
The faith we create in our mind
Will guarantee Heaven we can find

Faith gives us the power to be free
Seeking life's beauty, which is Heavenly.

****

Hebrews 11.1

'Faith is the assured expectation of things hoped for, the evident demonstration of realities though not beheld. '

Faith is always a positive belief system for the future good.

'When the Son of man arrives, will he really find the faith on Earth?' Luke: 18:8

Faith is always a positive goal.

Love is positive in the present.
Faith is positive belief in the future
Faith is Love being manifested.

There is no fear in Faith.

****

Revelation Sonnet

The Revelation Revolution is at hand
For surely God knows what is best for man
He says don't dim his light with sin
For surely sin will not benefit him

'When is doomsday' none can be sure
But maybe already there is a door
A door to open for man to see
How God's Love will become heavenly

The door only needs one special key
To make life perfect for you and for me
We need to polarize the spectrum of light
And shine the way forth for all to be right

The Light is shining bright forthwith
And commands consciousness of how Love forgives.

****

Human Rights

You say you want your rights
and demand rights for all, even the fallen
but how can you have rights when you are wrong,
and what determines wrongs and rights anyway?
Have you forgotten?

You demand your rights yet forget where they came from,
where is your grace? What is your humanity?

Maybe you didn't learn the origins in History
And maybe you fell asleep in RE
And maybe they did not teach the relevance
of History to prophecy, but to those who know
it is crystal clear
It is here before our very eyes today, if you can see.

So many demanding rights yet doing wrongs
Do you know the meaning of wrong and right,
Right and righteous, haram and halal?
Do you know why?

Do you know where the 'Hu' in human comes from anyway?

****

Big Ten

He says 'prevention is better than cure
with gratitude and grace
and if you don't actively listen
and adhere to my wisdom
there is a window for repentance
and from that repentance change
and from that change forgiveness with
reason, and understanding;
an apology allowing forgiveness
for consciousness and restoration
for joy to be restored'.

It works between all kinds
It works between all times
It works between all genders
It works between all neighbors

And at this resurrection time
when His gifts and presents are divine
remember the origin of all moral code
allowing us faith, love and peace
in our humble abodes.

Is His grace about to end?

****

My Body

(Your Body) Our Body's are the temple. 1 Corinthian 3:16

My body is my body, my beau where I exist
my temple where I worship, my castle where I live.

My body is my transport, my legs will take me far
my feet will take me dancing and walk to lands afar.

Afar my feet will walk with me as my heart talks with me
of the beauty that I see with my eyes that belong to me.

My body is my body I treasure it with Love
I feel it with my brain and heart and seek to find it's God.

My body is my body I treasure it with Light
I take it with me everywhere and sleep with it at night.

****

Christ Mass Eve Magic (Born to stable)

The twinkling excitement of anticipation with great expectation that causes insomnia on the one night when you want to go to sleep early to send your dreams and wishes bubbling forth like crisp, white snowflakes floating into the sky to the very clouds of hope that St Nicholas and his team of merry reindeer will descend through on the way to your house. Dreams of happiness and fulfillment creating warmth inside our hearts in the depth of ice dark winter; the shortest, darkest day turning the tide of light.

A sun in the moon, light - in the world comes from Positive Love of the greater good of others and self in a balanced measure giving peace and joy, warmth and well being.

The miraculous magic of goodwill born from righting the icicles of the cold north wind that pierces and freezes your faith. A gift of warmth and hope to get you to spring time like flames dancing up the chimney of hope that St Nicholas will descend to have a sherry and mince pie with Jesus, Mary and Joseph. The shepherds are with their flocks by night and the three kings from the Orient are travelling with their camels.

'So what are these gifts of Gold, Frankincense and Myrrh?' asks St Nicholas

'These are gifts for creating Positive Love' replies the Angel Gabriel.
'Love is always positive and kind, faithful and true,
it makes life worthwhile for you Gold is the most positive metal element.'

'And what of the oils of Frankincense and Myrrh?' St Nicholas asks again and the Angel replies

'Oh what oils to delight the soul and allay the fears to set your soul free for faith.

****

Frankincense lets love conquer fear, have no fear, only love and you can know the heaven above.

As for the Myrrh the most potent healing oil known at the time, antibacterial and antiseptic for bathing wounds and healing boils of the flesh.

These are the three most valuable gifts to overcome fear of death to create Love, Hope and Faith to stabilise Love and Faith in the physical world of mankind; to choose righteousness over sin, good over bad and truth over lies and betrayals for friendship unity and community for Heaven to materialise here on earth.' replies the Angel Gabriel.

'Jesus Christ' – 'The Anointed One who causes Love, His Father to become Love in us human beings on earth here and now for a world with Love, Joy, Peace and Happiness where there is no fear, no evil, no negativity and no stress to destabilise our emotional well being.

Have no fear, and Love conquers all'.

St Nicholas replies

'Well Ho, Ho, Ho, now I know why all this good cheer at this time of year. Happy Christ Mass and Happy New Year, Happy Holy Days, Holy Days (holidays) for all eternity.'

God blessed the world with Love through His Son created by Love, Anointed with a spirit of Love that is whole, holy manifesting in a Whole Positive Spirit of Peace for Peace and Positive Love and Light for the world.

'Let there be Light, let the Light of Love come to be'

Happy Christ Mass:

Unity with His Love.

****

Some philosophical thoughts on Religion;

Perhaps Jesus Christ was *born to stable,* stabilise our bodies in mind, body and spirit through His Love made whole in us to avoid the stress response caused by sin (done to or received by) by cultivating a clean conscience through self control and oneness through His Love made whole in us. I think so.

I wrote this poem because after my mother died on December 4th 1974 Christmas was never the same. However people's kindness to me at that time and the hope of Christmas and the excitement of Christmas Eve sustained my faith. I learned the excitement of expectation of good things and the hope of good things to come.

I realised fulfillment comes from the warmth generated from kindness in Love, but in the interim of having lost my mother's love, moderate Christmas celebrations were a good thing for me and are for many. In the northern hemispheres the cold and darkness can cause much isolation, depression, hypothermia and even death. Living in a small country village we had strong community values and still had our animals to tend to even on Christmas Day. For us Christmas gave a generous spirit of giving in dark times to warm the hearts and to kindle caring and loving relationships.'

'God loves a cheerful giver' and we can give at anytime, we do not need to wait for an occasion.

Later in life I learned 'expectation denied makes the heart sick' and we must learn balance of expectation and self respect and responsibility. The Golden Rule is perfection in this balance 'to Love God, others as self' not instead of self and this balanced measure gives the ultimate in Love for all. We must remember that 'God is Love' and a god is what we dedicate our time, intention and life too.

****

The poet Samuel Taylor Coleridge said 'Christian theology is only possible if both connection and reciprocal action are a priori factor.' As he demonstrates in his poem 'Rime of the Ancient Mariner' he believes we are spiritual beings with the ability to turn around from a wrong course of action and choose to do good. I think salvation of the positive life spirit of Love may only come from this altruistic conscious deed and action.

Coleridge also believed that philosophy is rooted in wonder and 'the true philosopher is a lover of God'. He held the imagination to be the living power and prime agent of all human perception and as a prepetition in the finite mind of the eternal act of creation in the infinite 'I AM'. He said 'to keep the mind in health it must be kept in exercise which is elaborate reasoning.' I agree with this but I do not think it is only empiricist, as in only reason, but that reason is applied to feelings good and bad as demonstrated in my poem Reasoning Love and this is the counseling process. TH Green attacks the empiricist view of the mind and utilitarian view of ethics and produces ethics of self realisation and the idea of God as 'one spiritual self conscious being which all that is real is the activity and expression. John Locke seems to have been the first Christian who ventured openly to assert that faith is nothing but a species of reason. The secure basis of Christianity is its reasonableness which is derived from the ethical core of Jesus' teaching. Hume attempts to show that morality is perfectly intelligible with out reference to metaphysical theism however spirit comes only from the Spirit of Love which is a biological system in us that can only be attained to with altruistic humility. God's perfect paradox I think.

From Coleridge, Philosophy and Religion by Douglas Hedley.

Similarly in his work The Reconstruction of Islamic Thought, Sir Muhhamad Iqbal speaks of knowledge and religious experience and transcending ego to attain to the true self, the spiritual nature of man which he calls Khudi., So that man 'will eventually triumph over a society motivated by an inhuman competition, and civilization which has lost its spiritual unity by its inner conflict of religious and political values.'

****

Ultimately if we can attain to fulfillment of ourselves to become the ethical things we love, and reason wrongs and hurts for repentance and forgiveness, then we can attain to that Oneness and Wholeness of spirit for fulfillment in all we do. Only then can we create peace and harmonious Love within to reflect without in all relationships thus creating two fold peace, within ourselves and without with others for peaceful and harmonious living for all as individuals and communities and nations. I do not think God wants us to be martyrs but wishes for us to choose to attain to the fullness of His Love made whole in us for His glory in Love to shine in us, all His human family enthused by His Love for harmonious living in peace together.

There is neither Jew nor Greek/ Gentile, neither slave nor free, nor is there male or female, for you are all one in Christ Jesus. Galatians 3:28 This Oneness is still relevant today.

When you see a Muslim person say to them 'Asalamu Alaikum' and see their eyes light up 'just as in the twinkling of an eye'. It is a beautiful greeting of peace and the response is 'Wa Alaykumu Asalam' which means 'and upon you peace'. A positive greeting will have been made. I think we are all human beings who respond to kindness to each other. Let's beat the drip fed terrorist fear and 'Islamophobia' (which in itself is a contradiction of terms as Islam means peace) with friendship and unity for peace and Love between us all. Let's focus and give glory to God, to the good, not the bad. I don't care how many newspapers it doesn't sell, but they may be surprised if they changed to positive news and cultivated an open and unified thinking culture for goodness with kindness.

****

Christ Mass Cake

Would you like a piece of my cake with your tea
a piece of my whole that is big enough to share with you
a piece of my Love to show my heart, to fill the hole of hunger
with sweet delight from a time when time was enough

to be almost full. A time when grace and gratitude prevailed in
smiles, fine bone china cups clinking, little fingers floating
etiquette not posh, but theatrical plays of perfection. An
act of Love when a time for peace was

time for a piece of cake with tea. This cake is offered round
and whole, a cake sweet with honey, nutritious with fruits
oozing port, almonds and cherries laced white with equilateral
pieces of a whole, cut to fill hunger eternally.

****

Gold (The most positively charged element.)

Golden days in golden haze of
golden rays and golden sands

Gold so much you can wear it
bathe it, put it on your face and

Crave it, building blocks of golden
towers showering golden flowers

No falters with gold,
stories yet to be told

Of life with gold.

'Buy from me Gold refined by fire'. Revelation 3:18

****

JBR Beach Song   Dubai

ting, ting, ting (hammers)
brrrrummmmm (cars)
woshsh woshshsh, woshsh woshshsh (sea, waves)
buzzzzzzzzzzz
brrrrummmmm
haaaaaaiiiiiahhhhh (call to prayer)
ting ting ting
bang bang bang (hammers)
dridridridridridridridri (drills)
ding dong ding dong ding dong (church bells ring)
hrrrruummmmmm
ding dong ding dong ding dong (church bells ring)
dridridridridridridri
bang bang bang (hammers)
haaaaaaiiiiahhhhh (call to prayer)
woshsh woshshsh, woshsh woshshsh
ting ting, ting

Faith respected.

****

Presence

Today is our present

Our present is a present

Only if and when we are present

And it can be pleasant

Life is His gift.

****

Love's Heart

A mirage around the body shimmering as heat on tarmac
at Roissy airport

An invisible dress of white linen veils, protecting

Sensing like a dog hunting, like the word doG in reverse

Radiating like a golden flower, blooming.

****

Thank God

I thank God for God, because man can be cruel
I thank God for dog because it is men and women that can be shite

I thank God for God because who else is there when all else fails;
who else is there when depths of despair deepen to depths

unfathomable, when life reaches only a point of prayer?
God; a real imaginary friend, dependable when all else fails.

Can God stop anyone choosing greed, betrayal or murder;
or would that contradict our gift of free will?

Can He teach us how to Love in mind, body and spirit:
to Love each other Positively and whole?

Whole in spirit, anointed fully with Love for Love to become
Whole; self actualisation

Creating Love for Love which is God in our presence,
Love in our present with Faith.

Who is God? Love, Light; Energy for enlightenment of Love
full brain thinking, full heart feeling, gut feelings made right .

Who else, what else makes us whole in perfection?
I thank God for Love made Golden in Turquoise Love.

****

A Modern Mariners' Tale

Inspired by Samuel Taylor Coleridge's poems The Rime of the Ancient Mariner'and Kubla Khan put to prophecies in The Book of Revelation

The modern mariner sets sail on his journey, liberties yet to be realised. Soul freedoms setting sail, heading into the flaming sun, ready to surf tidal waves to the refuge of a Kingdom with states of peaceful pleasures, pleasing the soul beyond measure. Yet storms gather;

Dark clouds cumulate and the winds whisk away oars so the broken vessels bob only in an ocean of faith, sitting on waters cascading light; Light leveling Loves' language, trusting in a new world; a pleasing dome of honest, moral truthful pleasures; 'The tent of God' with mankind;

Some vessels sink beneath waves, as lightening strikes hearts and thunder roars at the terror of the dragon breathing fireballs of destruction annihilating Love by burning mammals breasts and isolating babies like Lebensborn children. But the dragons' fireballs have no power in the sea of Love; fireballs of heartless, controlling sabotage will be dampened to sizzling steam whistling empty lies as they boil over in their fear, grief and anger; no pride in controlling fear led powers.

New waters on the horizon will be leveling equality to the humans being Love; the humans being loving beings, being human beings uniting in the messages of Love from above; to be kind in Love, the conscious power beyond the fish in the sea, the power that is heavenly, erupting from a new sea of Love's consciousness:

Volcanoes ignited erupting, spitting, spilling lava forming crystals to the sea of men to be kind: Man, kind in Love with eternal emeralds of peace, for peace for Love's wisdom emerging from faith as sapphires, courageous as jasper and rubies glowing like diamond lights dancing, chalcedony and topaz love placing righteous crowns on top of each and every mortals head;

Wars swallowed by the whale removing the wails of manmean, meanness, women or men being inhuman, Manmean; ragged, bloody, flesh torn limbs severed, blood seeping, wounds weeping, hearts weeping, eyes leaking please God

Reunite our hearts and minds to make whole the hearts of men and women, to make whole the body and blood of Christ: The Kingdom restored; 'Let Thy Kingdom come; Thy will be done on Earth as it is in Heaven';

Ideal ideals manifested for Heaven on Earth: New waters emerging as springs to feed the trees of life to be rife feeding the souls of men and women being kind uniting with trust and faith and empathy:

Whole food for lost souls to build a new body, new marrow, new bones, new blood nourishing states of peace of pleasures of health and wealth beyond measure for energy and utility;

Love and life free for eternity; man and woman being human beings; loving beings enthused to be kind in Love, this is the mind of Love; this is what we *owe the Albatross*.

****

Hippocratic Oath for World Peace

Inspired by Dylan Thomas's poem 'Do Not go Gentle into that Good Night'.

The World is filled with too much self loath
'rage, rage against the dying of the light'
shouldn't we all take the Hippocratic Oath?

'Not by bread alone' but give us our loaf
The Light has faded into a raging dark night
The World is filled with too much self loath.

World famine and greed, do you expect growth?
'do not go gentle into that good night'
shouldn't we all take the Hippocratic Oath?

People are starving and need a bread loaf
find joy, joy in the rising of The Light;
The World is filled with too much self loath.

Mix bread with l*es oeuf* for some fine toast;
a golden dawn of new light that is bright,
shouldn't we all take the Hippocratic Oath?

'Do not go gentle' into that dark night like most,
but find rapture for the coming of The Light
The World is filled with too much self loath,
We must all take the Hippocratic Oath.

Amen. Ameen. Shalom, Namaste.

****

'All Things New'

Revelation 21:3 'Look! The tent of God is with mankind and He will reside with them, and they will be his peoples. And God himself will be with them. 4 And he will wipe out every tear from their eyes, and death will be no more, neither will mourning nor outcry nor pain be anymore. The former things have passed away.'

5. And The One seated on the throne said: ' Look I am making all things new. Also he says: 'Write, because these words are faithful and true.' 6 And he said to me: 'They have come to pass! I am The Alpha and The Omega, the beginning and the end. To anyone thirsting I will give from the fountain of the water of life water free. 7 Anyone conquering will inherit these things, and I shall be his God and he will be my son.'

22:20 Yes I am coming quickly. Amen! Come Lord Jesus Come.

****

This book is my understanding of how God's Love took away my pain and healed my heart and mind through Faith in His Love being made whole in Love and fulfilling His promises.

As a professional Holistic therapist I found hands on therapies and ethical energy work and most especially Health Kinesiology and Touch for Health undeniable in the truth of how our bodies have been made. As I said previously, the perfect paradox of God that He has created us to honour and worship him humbly for our true fulfillment and happiness to abound in His spirit of Love made whole for all.

I have done my best for His Glory.

My job has been done. Now it is your choice.

Amen, Ameen, Shalom, Namaste.

****

End Notes

Dust to Dust and Returning Christ; Reference to vibrations and frequencies of Love, water and crystals are based on quantum physics and Masaru Emoto's work *'Messages from Water'* who demonstrates with photographs that human consciousness and emotions affect the molecular structure of water which raises the question do they affect us? His work explores water reacting differently to negative and positive thoughts, emotions and words demonstrating polluted water can be cleansed through prayer and positive visualization, though this is no reason to allow pollution of the water and the plastic pollution is a great sin against the sea and sea creatures. We are 70% water and resonate at different frequencies of emotion thereby creating molecular structures based on our feelings.

'I think therefore I am' Rene Descartes and Exodus 3.14 'I Am that I Am' or 'I SHALL PROVE TO BE WHAT I SHALL PROVE TO BE'.

'Adam, Eve and St Agnes' inspired by the name of Ivor Davies MBE first art happening event in the 1960s and his art piece of his grandfathers shot gun cut in half with the words 'do beat your swords into plowshares' from the book of Isaiah, 2:4. To 'Positively Die' book of Genesis 2.17, sometimes written as to 'surely die'.

'Positive Love' is a concept explored in my book Healing Poems for Positive Love and 'Book of Life' where Love by analysis of Love from physiology and scripture always has a positive psychological and physiological outcome.

'Il Paradiso' - Fresco commission won in a competition by Tintoretto in 1582, the grand finale of a vision of Paradise through Christ's Justice on Earth.

'Mammary Mountain' inspired by a Volcano painting by ... in Art Gallery in Santa Cruz on the volcanic Island of La Palma. First published in Indifaring Muse 2018.

****

'Parousia' meaning – the presence, arrival, official visit or the coming of Christ, the second coming for rapture, joy, bliss – Heaven on Earth.
'Parousia' poem - every cloud has a rainbow' Genesis 6:5-8 9:8-16 Revelation 10:1

'To be or not be Love' and 'Reasoning Love' are both inspired by William Shakespeare's quote 'to be or not to be, that is the question' from Hamlet, but applied in this case as tangible states of being which can only arise from Positive Love in the parasympathetic nervous system and whole brain function for creating endorphins by the experience of love.

'Revelation Sonnet' and 'Hurricane Shahid' quote 'when is doomsday?' from Agha Shahid Ali (1949 – 2001) 'Today, talk is cheap. Call Somebody.' And 'A Ghazal' and 'Hurricane Shahid' inspired by 'Tonight' 'After You' 'Even the Rain' and 'In Arabic' from his collection 'Call me Ishmael Tonight' on the theme of exile and adoption which has perhaps influenced this whole collection.
In 'A Ghazal'; a Pharin is a long wool cloak worn in Kashmir and a kangris is a hot coal pot kept under the pharin.

'The End' published in Roath writers Anthology To the Pub and Back V 2017 Anandamide is the bliss molecule, oxytocin the neuro chemical allowing bonding and emotional attachments, serotonin an antidepressant and dopamine a reward and relaxant.

I Am: The One; Love – Exodus 3:14 and inspired by Sir Muhammad Iqbal (1877 - 1938) concept of Khudi and Samuel Taylor Coleridge (1772 -1834) Self actualization through reason. Published Gloucester Poetry Society.

A Modern Mariners Tale inspired by Samuel Taylor Coleridge's Rime of the Ancient Mariner and Kubla Kahn was first performed in National Museum of Wales as part of Coleridge in Wales Project 2016.

Hippocratic Oath written at Dylan Thomas Centre and used as part of Dylan Thomas Day in Cardiff central library.

****

Water Levels of Consciousness and Water Mark published in The Angry Manifesto.

Gold and JBR Beach Song from Blending Oil and Water collection written in Dubai.

The Heavenly City: Zion 'reached the height of Everest' Tawqeer Mir

Amen means So be it, and derived from Hebrew for certainty, truth.
Ameen is Amen in Arabic and as an assent of others prayers and also a name meaning faithful and trustworthy.
Shalom is a Hebrew greeting or parting meaning peace which means to be safe in mind, body and estate, and speaks of completeness, wholeness and tranquility with giving back.
Namaste is a bow gesture of respect and gratitude to the divine spark within our heart chakra - the chakra of Divine Love.
As-salamu Alaikum Arabic greeting meaning peace be upon you.

Most Bible references from New World translation of The Holy Scriptures including God's name.

Many poems published on my social media channels.

Pamphlet length of this collection long listed with Cinnamon Press 2017, other collections also Long listed with Cinnamon Press;
Blending Oil and Water 2016
Hiraeth Kynnersley 2017.

****

Additional Thoughts

Bread of Heaven; He Who Causes Love to Become Whole; JHVH YHWH Yashua; Anointed with the Whole, Holy Spirit: One Love Jesus Christ manifested in us. Revelation 21: New Jerusalem; New Heavens, 'The Crystal Fountain' for 'healing pain', The Re Gathering of the tribes of Israel: 144,000 states of being causing Love to become whole in us for resurrecting and manifesting a whole spirit of Positive Love worthy of honour for Love and Peace on Earth, the putting on of incorruption, change of heart for others good, 'just as in the twinkling of an eye'. 1st Corinthians 15:51-2 Isaiah 9:6: 'For there has been a child born to us, there has been a son given to us, and his name will be called 'Wonderful Counsellor, Mighty God, Eternal Father, Prince of Peace' Isaiah 9.6: Love made whole is the reason for and to heal.

Healing of pain for peace on earth through the whole spirit of Love that is positive in man for Kindness; + Positive Love, Faith, Discernment, Righteous, Consciousness, Friendship, Unity, Communion; so be it - literally for Peace & Love with Heaven manifested on Earth. War no more, kill no more, create the beauty in life for all; so be it, Be Love, to be Love is the answer, the Light of understanding with reason for justice and creating trust, security and peace, One God who causes Love to become whole, anointed with His whole Spirit for Ephraim; doubly fruitful results internal and external for All Nations to heal pain.

In accord with this measure of pure righteousness and forgiveness for Love and Peace to prevail for health and healing would it be right to adopt Ishmael back into the tribe in accordance with his first born rights and possibly bring lasting peace between the three main monotheistic faiths? Ishmael - He who listens to God, Allah is the title for One God in Arabic, Islam means peace and a Muslim is someone who submits their will to God. I am now reading the Quran because my Muslim friends demonstrate many fruits of the spirit to me, perhaps more so than some so called Christians but there is no division in Gods eyes of His people devout in Love and fear of the One God of Love and merciful kindness.

****

Maybe then there can be a healing for *All Nations* for Man to become Kind in His Whole Love for Peace. So Be It.

God willing in English, Insh Allah in Arabic. Amen. Ameen, Shalom, Namaste.

Unity, Communion, Friendship, Consciousness, Righteous, Discernment, Faith, Love which are always positive for all.
Amen, Ameen, Shalom, Namaste.

JHVH: He who causes Love to become Jesus Christ: Anointed One made whole in the spirit of Love Whole Spirit of Love manifested in us for men/women to become Whole in spirit for the fruits of the spirit for Love to become; 'Love, Joy, Peace, long suffering, kindness, goodness, faith, mildness, self control. Against such things there is no law. Galatians 5:22. Contrast with the previous verses describing the works of the flesh made manifest ' and they are fornication, uncleanness, loose conduct, idolatry, practice of spiritism, enmities, strife, jealously, fits of anger, contentions, divisions, sects, envies, drunken bouts, revelries, and such things like these…those who practice such things will not inherit God's kingdom.' Galatians 19 -22 I think drugs and all sin comes into such 'things like these' because they are all causing stress in our body systems and toxicity which needs to be detoxified and cleansed for health, healing and well being. Fleshly traits describe erratic stress hormones which can cause havoc to our health and well being. Stress is the root of every disease and all stress is fear reaction whether conscious or not so it is our duty to cultivate love for avoidance of sin for our own and others well being for a positive life for all.

"By the fruits we will know them." Matthew 7. 15 -20

Love to become whole to Love God and others as self for heaven on earth for rapture of the spirit of love for love in man to become kind.

****

There is only One Love made whole by submission to God's Love for Love to prevail for Joy and Peace in man on Earth for a healing for All Nations. Amen. Ameen. Shalom, Namaste.

22:7 And look! I am coming quickly...Amen.

Cup of Positive Love

Unity

Friendship

Consciousness

Righteousness

Discernment

Faith

Love

The 7 Foundations - Pillars for Making Love Whole
discerned from The Bible Book of Revelation chapters 2 and 3 messages to the 7 congregations.

****

Revelation 21: The New Jerusalem

12 positive thoughts x 12 positive thoughts applied to every grievance, pain or irritation in mind, body and spirit becomes 144 Positive thoughts to conquer sin in mind 0, body 0,and spirit 0 for a whole 0 Spirit to remove pain by repentance and forgiveness to create happiness and Love made whole in us for Peace. So be Love and let Love's Light shine brightly for healing Love to become manifest for All Nations.

Jasper Judah Courage	Sapphire Reuben Faith	Chalcedony Gad Happiness	Emerald Asher Peace	Sardonyx Naphtali Wrestlings understand	Sardius Manasseh Forgive	Chrysolite Simeon Hear	Beryl Levi Adherence	Topaz Issachar Reward	Chrysoprase Zebulun Tolerance	Hyacinth Joseph Trust	Amethyst Ben Truth
Sapphire Reuben Faith	Chalcedony Gad Happiness	Emerald Asher Peace	Sardonyx Naphtali Wrestlings understand	Sardius Manasseh Forgive	Chrysolite Simeon Hear	Beryl Levi Adherence	Topaz Issachar Reward	Chrysoprase Zebulun Tolerance	Hyacinth Joseph Trust	Amethyst Ben Truth	Jasper Judah Courage
Chalcedony Gad Happiness	Emerald Asher Peace	Sardonyx Naphtali Wrestlings understand	Sardius Manasseh Forgive	Chrysolite Simeon Hear	Beryl Levi Adherence	Topaz Issachar Reward	Chrysoprase Zebulun Tolerance	Hyacinth Joseph Trust	Amethyst Ben Truth	Jasper Judah Courage	Sapphire Reuben Faith
Emerald Asher Peace	Sardonyx Naphtali Wrestlings understand	Sardius Manasseh Forgive	Chrysolite Simeon Hear	Beryl Levi Adherence	Topaz Issachar Reward	Chrysoprase Zebulun Tolerance	Hyacinth Joseph Trust	Amethyst Ben Truth	Jasper Judah Courage	Sapphire Reuben Faith	Chalcedony Gad Happiness
Sardonyx Naphtali Wrestlings understand	Sardius Manasseh Forgive	Chrysolite Simeon Hear	Beryl Levi Adherence	Topaz Issachar Reward	Chrysoprase Zebulun Tolerance	Hyacinth Joseph Trust	Amethyst Ben Truth	Jasper Judah Courage	Sapphire Reuben Faith	Chalcedony Gad Happiness	Emerald Asher Peace
Sardius Manasseh Forgive	Chrysolite Simeon Hear	Beryl Levi Adherence	Topaz Issachar Reward	Chrysoprase Zebulun Tolerance	Hyacinth Joseph Trust	Amethyst Ben Truth	Jasper Judah Courage	Sapphire Reuben Faith	Chalcedony Gad Happiness	Emerald Asher Peace	Sardonyx Naphtali Wrestlings understand
Chrysolite Simeon Hear	Beryl Levi Adherence	Topaz Issachar Reward	Chrysoprase Zebulun Tolerance	Hyacinth Joseph Trust	Amethyst Ben Truth	Jasper Judah Courage	Sapphire Reuben Faith	Chalcedony Gad Happiness	Emerald Asher Peace	Sardonyx Naphtali Wrestlings understand	Sardius Manasseh Forgive
Beryl Levi Adherence	Topaz Issachar Reward	Chrysoprase Zebulun Tolerance	Hyacinth Joseph Trust	Amethyst Ben Truth	Jasper Judah Courage	Sapphire Reuben Faith	Chalcedony Gad Happiness	Emerald Asher Peace	Sardonyx Naphtali Wrestlings understand	Sardius Manasseh Forgive	Chrysolite Simeon Hear
Topaz Issachar Reward	Chrysoprase Zebulun Tolerance	Hyacinth Joseph Trust	Amethyst Ben Truth	Jasper Judah Courage	Sapphire Reuben Faith	Chalcedony Gad Happiness	Emerald Asher Peace	Sardonyx Naphtali Wrestlings to understand	Sardius Manasseh Forgive	Chrysolite Simeon Hear	Beryl Levi Adherence
Chrysoprase Zebulun Tolerance	Hyacinth Joseph Trust	Amethyst Ben Truth	Jasper Judah Courage	Sapphire Reuben Faith	Chalcedony Gad Happiness	Emerald Asher Peace	Sardonyx Naphtali Wrestlings to understand	Sardius Manasseh Forgive	Chrysolite Simeon Hear	Beryl Levi Adherence	Topaz Issachar Reward
Hyacinth Joseph Trust	Amethyst Ben Truth	Jasper Judah Courage	Sapphire Reuben Faith	Chalcedony Gad Happiness	Emerald Asher Peace	Sardonyx Naphtali Wrestlings to understand	Sardius Manasseh Forgive	Chrysolite Simeon Hear	Beryl Levi Adherence	Topaz Issachar Reward	Chrysoprase Zebulun Tolerance
Amethyst Ben Truth	Jasper Judah Courage	Sapphire Reuben Faith	Chalcedony Gad Happiness	Emerald Asher Peace	Sardonyx Naphtali Wrestlings to understand	Sardius Manasseh Forgive	Chrysolite Simeon Hear	Beryl Levi Adherence	Topaz Issachar Reward	Chrysoprase Zebulun Tolerance	Hyacinth Joseph Trust

Nothing added, nothing taken away just Love's Light concluded and translated into a universal language of Love for a healing of *All Nations*. Amen, Ameen, Shalom, Namaste.

Love's Light Sealed Revelation (7 & 21).

****

Courage to **seek** true **happiness** and face pain and fears, to turn away from sin, and betrayals; haram with **faith** in a Positive outcome for all; halal for **peace** with in and with out, with self and with others and God, overcoming the **wrestlings** between good and bad, right and wrong for **righteousness** to **forgive** (if necessary) and **actively listen** standing firm in **faith** for the **heavenly reward** and fulfillment for tolerance of others, find **trust** and seek truth for a quiet conscience and **peace** of mind. Have the great **courage** to **turn away from sin** to **seek happiness** with **Faith** in **Happiness**, **Wrestling**'s to **Forgive**, to **Actively Listen**, **Hear**, **Adhere**, for the endorphin **Reward** with **Tolerance** and **Truth**, **Trust** for **two fold Peace** within and without when we **listen and submit our will to God** who is **Love** and **Light** and always **Positive.**
Thank you to God for my Faith in Him and His Love and promises of healing and may Jesus Christ come quickly and fulfill His promise for removing pain for a healing for *All Nations* and bring Peace on Earth, Heaven brought down to Earth by Love made Whole in us to give freely with **righteousness fulfilled** through **Faith** and **Love** in us.

Sin is Anti Christ; Sin is stress, guilt, shame and fear; a falling short of Love; Sin is against Love; in opposition to Love in our nervous system. Sin creates adrenaline and cortisols in our blood.
Could Sin be The AntiChrist?
Love is not a cortisol, Love has an endorphin blood.
May Love conquer fear for Love, peace and security to prevail for happiness in making men and women kind. So be Love. Amen, Ameen, Shalom, Namaste.

****

Call for Peace

In the Name of God of 'the one who causes Love to become whole in the Positive Spirit of Love and Faith made whole in us' I call to the politicians and world leaders to call for Love, Peace and Security for all life on Earth by means of Peace treaties for disarmament with understanding the mindset of God's Love made whole and complete in us to create Peace within ourselves and Peace without with others for Peace with the God who is Love and Peace for *All Nations*. We can all be prophets of Peace and sons (and daughters) of God with His Love made Whole in us by turning away from all sin. Rev 21:7

There can only be One Almighty God of Love and Mercy for Love and Light, positive energy for all for fulfillment of a Whole Spirit of Love with all the fruits of the spirit namely Love, Joy, Peace, Patience, Kindness, Goodness, Faith, Mildness with Self Control for Honesty, Integrity, Trust and Security in Life Against such things there is no law. Galatians 5:22.

With consciousness illuminated and embraced by organizational governments there is no need for fear of fleshly conflict anymore and with generosity of spirit and investment of the peoples funds (if money still exists) in the people and planet then there is no place for weapons, hunger, dirty water or poverty anymore. With these basic and true human rights and health improvements, hunger, disease, pestilence and famine will be eradicated as will death of the spirit of Love. With Love prevailing life will be energized and perhaps even life spans extended.

****

I believe this is Faithfull and True; The Heavenly City descended to Earth, The New Jerusalem for two fold Peace on Earth for paradise to be restored for rapture of our spirit of Love made whole in us for the whole spirit of Love and Peace which we are all seeking for a healing of All Nations and for The Promised Land of Heaven to come down to Earth.

Come and take life's water freely, Come Lord Jesus Christ with the Whole Spirit for us all to live together with Love, Faith, Peace and Harmony for all. 'Come Lord Jesus Come, He is coming quickly' Revelation 22. .

God Willing in English,
Insh Allah in Arabic.
As-salamu Alaikum,

Amen, Ameen, Shalom, Namaste.

I have given my all, I have done my best.
The rest is up to God.

****

Acknowledgements

Thank you to my One God of One Love who causes Love to become YHWH, JHVH and His Son Jesus Christ who makes Love whole in the whole Spirit of One Love in us, the name Allah is a title for One God and is as I understand the Arabic name for the One God of Love from the Old Testament. Jesus said 'by their fruits we will know them' and I see many good fruits in many people and organizations. Islam means peace and peace is a fruit of the spirit of Love made whole in us. A Muslim is a person who submits their will to Allah - a title meaning The One God. Let there be Light and may Love come to be for a healing for *All Nations* through unity of a positive spirit of Love manifested in man to become kind throughout our world.

Thank you to my family whom I love very much and thank you for their patience and tolerance of my work which they have not fully understood. Thank you to the financial support of my ex husband and his company. Thank you to all my friends who have demonstrated their love, faith and support throughout my life, especially Debs, Karen, Karena, Jenny, Kate, Sarah and Annie. To my wonderful mum Beryl and her mum, my Nana; Jessie Moore and to my dad Roy Williams and the 'Godly village of Kynnersley' where I was welcomed and embraced by everyone which gave me such a secure foundation and strong faith by example to base my life on (quote from Hiraeth Kynnersely poetry collection). My lifelong friends Penny and Patsy, auntie Joan and Mrs Boot who stood by me at a time of need. Thank you to my faithful God Mothers who have remained faithful in my life.

Thank you to Pauline Williams for inviting me to travel with her to visit these wonderful faith fulfilling places and her belief in me on my poetry journey and thank you to her for beautiful illustrations and paintings which are the covers of Healing Poems for Positive Love, Book of Life and Apocalyptic Poem. Also thank you for introducing me to the Renaissance Art in the magnificent European Churches and museums. I see them as a fine witness to the scriptures and The Book of Revelation in themselves. It is true a picture paints a thousand words, and in this case the pictures paint thousands of words of vices, virtues and hope.

Equally the simplicity of a small country church is as endearing to me and I also love to commune with God in nature, the sea and Light and when walking my dogs or riding horses. It is true He is everywhere, we find Him where 'two or more are gathered in Jesus' name'; in the whole spirit of Love with faith. Love is our truth for finding peace and joy.

I thank my dogs for their endless patience while I take photographs and write on our walks and with a special memory for Bruce – 'the mighty little dog' who shared this journey and my cats Pushkin 2 and Black Knight who sat with me though endless nights of writing. Thank you to Claire for Koty who helped sustain my need for a horse in my life and all the joy of being at the stables.

****

Thank you to the YouTube eschatologists namely Scottie Clarke, Gevte, One Point Preparedness, Adam at Parable of the Vineyard, and friends and recommended channels and many more. Thank you to Paul Wilbur's beautiful, beautiful worship songs, the evident passion for Christ of Rise on Fire and many more. I could not listen to everyone. A remembrance to Billy Graham who died this week 21/2/18 who it seems to me was a man with great faith and calling for repentance from sin and converting many to Christ. Thank to Untold History by Merciful Servant and to Kashmir and I and other Islam channels and so many good channels of information, too many to mention. Thank you for my study with Jehovah's Witnesses, to my local Churches and community and to Brother Paul and The Church of New Hope in Africa and to *all* who spread the message of Love through Faith in The One God of Love and mercy who makes us whole in Love. There are very, very, very many good and faithful people cultivating love and peace in every righteous organization and of course all thanks be to God who is Love.

Thank you to Sian Fox at Foxy's Delicatessen for hosting our poetry evenings and to my poet and musician friends who have been a support and part on this journey - Julie Pritchard, Bel Blue, Fritz O'Skennick Richard Parry, Chris Glyn, Aled Hughes, Rufus Mufasa, Kevs Ford, Dave Daggers, Will Ford, Mark Curtis, Brian Marshall, Laz, Bridget and Paula, and all at RARA , Rhyme and Real Ale at The Macintosh Sports and Racket Club in Roath, Roath Writers, Amy Wack and Seren Books First Thursday at Chapter, Alan Roderick and The Murenger Poets; Bernard Pearson, Jonathon Edwards, Angela and Greg Platt and photographer John Briggs; Renn at Juke; Ziggy and Jason at The Gloucester Poetry Society, Matt Duggan and Simon editors of The Angry Manifesto, Rob, Fiona and Cara Cullen from Voices from the Bridge, and all my local open mics and music venues; Hank at The Look Out Bar, Rob at the Ex Servicemen's Club and Tony at The Albion where many a woe has been danced into joy and celebration with friends and music and new friends made. Thank you to Reuben Woolley at *I am not a silent poet,* online publication, to Des Mannay, Adam Johannes, Mab Jones, Amanda Rackstraw, Sue Morgan and Bob Walton for their encouragement and to everyone who has listened to me reading and spoken words of constructive criticism and appreciation to help me on my poetic journey.

Thank you to my many, many clients over thirty years who have been a big part of my understanding the emotional aspects of healing and restoring of health and well being through self actualization for healing pain to regain vibrant energy for a positive life.

Thanks to Doug Dalwood for help with editing and recognizing the therapeutic, scientific and theological aspects of my work. Thank you to Jan Fortune, Adam Craig, Peter Marshall and fellow poets on the wonderful Cinnamon Press courses where I worked on honing and editing some of the European poems and thank you to Rich and Christina Thatcher for helping with the publishing process.

Thank you to the ship and crew of Oceana and Ventura who looked after me so well and helped restore my wellbeing at a time of need.

Thank you to NHS, MIND, The Women's Centre Cardiff, Banardos, Re- Live Choir, Marcos, Annie, Helen, Hellena and John who all helped restore my well being with holistic therapies when my arm seized. I knew it was stuck grief.

Thank you to Re-Live Choir and special remembrance for our dear friend Hamish who could not cope with the pain and trauma he lived with. And thank you to my local ladies choir I recently joined. I find singing such a connection to the self and others and the divine. Singing in a choir is resonance of pure joy. With special memory to my school friends; Harry Mellor, Heather Blatcher and Frances Andrade who was not emotionally or psychologically supported enough during her tragic abuse trial.

Thank you to Sally Uphill photography for my Healing poems author photo and to John Briggs and Dave Daggers for many poetry images, thank you Maryna for doing my website and to Iryna for her belief in my work..

****

Thank you to my dear friend and 'adopted son' Tawqeer (of Indian Kashmir) for firstly his encouragement and belief in my poetry and for allaying misunderstandings and educating me to peaceful truths of Islam and helping me understand some Muslim belief systems for peace and love. Thank you also for introducing me to the Eastern poets; Sir Muhammad Iqbal, Agha Shahid Ali, Lal Ded and Rabindranath Tagore. Agha Shahid Ali's work in particular influenced and inspired my poems A Ghazal, Kashmir Snow and Hurricane Shahid and his collection 'Call me Ishmael Tonight' has been a strong influence. All this inspired my poem Building Bridges: One Love. The experiences of adoption, inheritance and exile inspired the connection and re--gathering ideas for Israel to include Ishmael , it is like a family healing, a welcoming home for a lost son for a healing of *all nations* for faith and love to be restored for all to heal and unite in The Oneness of Love who is God- I hope and pray; God willing in English, Insh Allah in Arabic - a common phrase Tawqeer and I used in many of our conversations.

Thank you to my multi cultural lady friends from WMAD and to those who have embraced Healing Poems for Positive Love and thank you to my friend Mohammed from Ely for respecting Healing Poems for Positive Love enough to want to translate into Arabic.

Thank you to Idania and Louise for teaching me to dance salsa and improve confidence in moving my body and all our dancing and musical friends.

.

Thank you to all my teachers of scripture and healing and creative writing and poetry but of course in truth - 'there is only one teacher'.

All thanks and glory be to God.

****

Thank you to the God of Love for my Faith in God and Jesus Christ's promise of healing and may He come quickly and fulfill His promise for removing pain and a healing for *All Nations* and bring unity through faith and Love for peace on Earth, Heaven brought down to Earth.
Amen. Ameen. Shalom, Namaste.

I think sin is the Anti Christ.

May Love conquer fear for Love, joy, peace, patience, kindness, goodness, faith with self control for Love, joy, peace, patience, kindness, goodness, faith with self control for trust, faith and security to prevail for peace and happiness in mankind, for Heaven to come down to Earth to restore our potential to live in the promise of paradise; Heaven on Earth. We have the duty to create this paradise with His Love made Whole in us for fruitage of His spirit made whole in us. Amen. Ameen. Shalom, Namaste. So be Love.

****

Crystal Fountain

Open now the crystal fountain 'William Williams.

Revelation 21: New Jerusalem; Mount Zion for healing pain and creating a whole spirit of Love: 'He Who Causes Love to Become' Whole; JHVH, YAWH,

Yashua anointed with the whole, Holy Spirit:

One Love; Jesus Christ manifested in us.

The Re Gathering of The Tribes of Israel:

144,000 states of conscious being causing Love to become whole in us for resurrecting and manifesting a whole spirit of Positive Love worthy of honour for Love and Peace on Earth;

The 'putting on of in corruption' a change of heart for others good, 'just as in the twinkling of an eye' 1st Corinthians 15:51-2

'For there has been a child born to us, there has been a Son given to us, and his name will be called 'Wonderful Counsellor, Mighty God, Eternal Father, Prince of Peace' Isaiah 9:6:

12 x12 = 144,000 + thoughts for avoiding sin and creating

Love

Made whole which is always positive.

$E = MC^2$ = Mass/Flesh x speed of Love/Light for Energy

for resonance of Positive Love and Life in us.

Amen, Ameen, Shalom, Namaste.

****

A New Heaven Translated

Everything real is invisible; gifts of Rubies (courage) transformed from Pearls (irritations),

Emeralds (peace) made from Sapphires squared(faith),

Attaining to Amethysts shining (truth) like diamonds dancing delicately on water.

Chalcedony waltzing (happiness) with Topaz (the endorphin reward)

Sardonyx serenading (wrestling's to understand) Sardius (for forgiveness)

Turquoise (trust and protection) passions speaking Love;

Love made whole like an O livine (full life)
fulfilling, complete, like a mine of treasures with no dragon, No pirates or opposition,

Just understanding with reason,

Chrysolite gold molten (active listening) into an
Emerald river (of peace) flowing to a
Chrysoprase (tolerant) sea.

****

The Holy City; Heavenly New Jerusalem for Heaven to come to Earth. 144,000 thoughts and states of being for creating the Whole Spirit of Love, Joy, Faith, Patience, Goodness, Mildness, Kindness, with Self Control for Peace in our thoughts, in Heaven and on Earth with self and others for two fold peace sealed.
Amen. Ameen. Shalom, Namaste.

Jasper Judah Courage	Sapphire Reuben Faith	Chalcedony Gad Happiness	Emerald Asher Peace	Sardonyx Naphtali Wrestlings understand	Sardius Manasseh Forgive	Chrysolite Simeon Hear	Beryl Levi Adherence	Topaz Issachar Reward	Chrysoprase Zebulun Tolerance	Hyacinth Joseph Trust	Amethyst Ben Truth
Sapphire Reuben Faith	Chalcedony Gad Happiness	Emerald Asher Peace	Sardonyx Naphtali Wrestlings understand	Sardius Manasseh Forgive	Chrysolite Simeon Hear	Beryl Levi Adherence	Topaz Issachar Reward	Chrysoprase Zebulun Tolerance	Hyacinth Joseph Trust	Amethyst Ben Truth	Jasper Judah Courage
Chalcedony Gad Happiness	Emerald Asher Peace	Sardonyx Naphtali Wrestlings understand	Sardius Manasseh Forgive	Chrysolite Simeon Hear	Beryl Levi Adherence	Topaz Issachar Reward	Chrysoprase Zebulun Tolerance	Hyacinth Joseph Trust	Amethyst Ben Truth	Jasper Judah Courage	Sapphire Reuben Faith
Emerald Asher Peace	Sardonyx Naphtali Wrestlings understand	Sardius Manasseh Forgive	Chrysolite Simeon Hear	Beryl Levi Adherence	Topaz Issachar Reward	Chrysoprase Zebulun Tolerance	Hyacinth Joseph Trust	Amethyst Ben Truth	Jasper Judah Courage	Sapphire Reuben Faith	Chalcedony Gad Happiness
Sardonyx Naphtali Wrestlings understand	Sardius Manasseh Forgive	Chrysolite Simeon Hear	Beryl Levi Adherence	Topaz Issachar Reward	Chrysoprase Zebulun Tolerance	Hyacinth Joseph Trust	Amethyst Ben Truth	Jasper Judah Courage	Sapphire Reuben Faith	Chalcedony Gad Happiness	Emerald Asher Peace
Sardius Manasseh Forgive	Chrysolite Simeon Hear	Beryl Levi Adherence	Topaz Issachar Reward	Chrysoprase Zebulun Tolerance	Hyacinth Joseph Trust	Amethyst Ben Truth	Jasper Judah Courage	Sapphire Reuben Faith	Chalcedony Gad Happiness	Emerald Asher Peace	Sardonyx Naphtali Wrestlings understand
Chrysolite Simeon Hear	Beryl Levi Adherence	Topaz Issachar Reward	Chrysoprase Zebulun Tolerance	Hyacinth Joseph Trust	Amethyst Ben Truth	Jasper Judah Courage	Sapphire Reuben Faith	Chalcedony Gad Happiness	Emerald Asher Peace	Sardonyx Naphtali Wrestlings understand	Sardius Manasseh Forgive
Beryl Levi Adherence	Topaz Issachar Reward	Chrysoprase Zebulun Tolerance	Hyacinth Joseph Trust	Amethyst Ben Truth	Jasper Judah Courage	Sapphire Reuben Faith	Chalcedony Gad Happiness	Emerald Asher Peace	Sardonyx Naphtali Wrestlings understand	Sardius Manasseh Forgive	Chrysolite Simeon Hear
Topaz Issachar Reward	Chrysoprase Zebulun Tolerance	Hyacinth Joseph Trust	Amethyst Ben Truth	Jasper Judah Courage	Sapphire Reuben Faith	Chalcedony Gad Happiness	Emerald Asher Peace	Sardonyx Naphtali Wrestlings to understand	Sardius Manasseh Forgive	Chrysolite Simeon Hear	Beryl Levi Adherence
Chrysoprase Zebulun Tolerance	Hyacinth Joseph Trust	Amethyst Ben Truth	Jasper Judah Courage	Sapphire Reuben Faith	Chalcedony Gad Happiness	Emerald Asher Peace	Sardonyx Naphtali Wrestlings to understand	Sardius Manasseh Forgive	Chrysolite Simeon Hear	Beryl Levi Adherence	Topaz Issachar Reward
Hyacinth Joseph Trust	Amethyst Ben Truth	Jasper Judah Courage	Sapphire Reuben Faith	Chalcedony Gad Happiness	Emerald Asher Peace	Sardonyx Naphtali Wrestlings to understand	Sardius Manasseh Forgive	Chrysolite Simeon Hear	Beryl Levi Adherence	Topaz Issachar Reward	Chrysoprase Zebulun Tolerance
Amethyst Ben Truth	Jasper Judah Courage	Sapphire Reuben Faith	Chalcedony Gad Happiness	Emerald Asher Peace	Sardonyx Naphtali Wrestlings to understand	Sardius Manasseh Forgive	Chrysolite Simeon Hear	Beryl Levi Adherence	Topaz Issachar Reward	Chrysoprase Zebulun Tolerance	Hyacinth Joseph Trust

Nothing added, nothing taken away; just The Word translated into the universal language of Love.
'A picture paints a thousand words'
144,000 words for Love made whole;
Oneness in Love, there is only One Love.
I trust this is Faithful and True.

****

I have faith this is Faithful and True and 'Look''I am coming quickly' for peace and security for a healing of 'All Nations' perhaps with forgiveness and adoption of a lost son 'who listens to God' back to the tribe for a family healing in accord with His perfect Love.

God Willing in English
Insha Allah in Arabic.

In the name of Jesus Christ our Lord and saviour: Love made Whole in us through the whole spirit of Love made whole in us for oneness in Love, Oneness, wholeness, complete

Amen. Ameen, Shalom, Namaste.

The End is the beginning of the word Endorphin; perhaps The Blood of Christ made whole in us.

****

****

Author Biography

With 30 years studying and working with the healing arts as a Holistic Therapist, Francess identifies emotional links between mind, body and spirit. In her work she explores boundaries of love and fear physiologically and emotionally and has had great success in her therapy practice with humans and animals.

After the Kinesiology technique of muscle testing was challenged by some religious individuals as a form of divination based on the scriptures saying 'those that are practicing fornication, spiritism, divination, and such things will not inherit the Kingdom of God' Fran focused her studies on the healing message of God who is Love and Light and set out to find out what made Jesus Christ the greatest healer of all time. Knowing that professional muscle testing is not divination nor is any spiritism being practiced when muscle testing is applied ethically and professionally.

Kinesiology is working with the intelligent system of the whole body based on the cell's innate sense of intelligence which goes beyond our intellectual suppositions. Fran found that pain and trauma were at the root of most ailments she worked with and realised that many problems originated with betrayals of love and trust or things classed as sin. Having great faith in a God of Love who fulfills His promises to all to 'remove pain' she found pain could be removed successfully.

Francess conveys these understandings in her books and poetry with great appreciation for the miracle of life in the human body and demonstrates contrasting states of love, stress and fear as tangible states of being and directs all praise and glory to Our Father and Almighty Creator God of Love.

****

From the stars to the star fish and Genesis to Revelation her work addresses all in between to inspire love and kindness for a healing for all for happiness, joy and peace on earth.

Publications include:

Healing Poems for Positive Love (2012) - available from Amazon.co.uk Frances Smith- Williams

Book of Life – a summary of the thesis in Healing Poems for Positive Love available on kindle and soon on Amazon.

Ultimate Healing Poems - Audio CD - some available on her You Tube for free Frances Smith @ Healing Poems.
Face book Fran Smith @ Healing Poems.

Lost Loves - A poetry pamphlet to help complete the grieving process. Makes a thoughtful and lasting sympathy gift with a therapeutic application of words.

Publications include *I Am Not a Silent Poet, London Poetry Grip, The Angry Manifesto, Penarth Times*, BBC Radio Wales, Cardiff Radio, Anthologies of Roath Writers, RARA and RVLF, *Domestic Cherry Magazine, Indifaring Muse, Saravasti Magazine, professional magazine*.

Social action projects:
Forget Me Knot campaign to raise awareness of modern day slavery .
Hidden Now Heard – Disability Wales Mental Health project,
Peace poems for Armistice Day.
Multi Faith Winter Celebration and many social justice events.

****

Francess specialises in holistic techniques for the reduction of stress, pain and PTSD with people, animals and horses for personal, bespoke sessions and is available for workshops, festivals, performance, talks and poetry readings.

You tube Frances Smith @ Healing Poems

Facebook Fran Smith @ Healing Poems

Twitter @ Healing Poems

Instagram Healing Poems.

But I am not very social media savvy or coordinated - yet.

****

Some Anonymous Praises

'A delightful read'

'A very soothing, inspiring and quiet spiritual journey. As I travel a lot I enjoy having your book with me as a friend to rely on, it helps me to focus and connect with my emotions and feeds my energy and soul .'

'You have brought everything together, perfectly'

'A wonderful inspiring journey'.

'I would like to visit these destinations with this book'.

'I haven't viewed it like this before, it makes perfect sense.'

'So true'.

'I am back in Venice - you have captured the essence of Venice perfectly.'

'The Bible Nuggeted - into Gold'

'Profound'

****

The End

The end is the start of the beginning of the word endorphin
the end of the quest for heart smiles in Love
mimicked by opium posing as opiates
killing pain knowing pleasure
addictive, seductive, seducing
ending enslavement to cortisols crying for an end,
the end; the release of endorphins
the dopamine, the serotonin, the oxytocin , the anandamide
binding the blood in marriage with Love
which is always positive
the endorphin is the end
the end is the beginning of The Word; Endorphin;
His Love in our blood
the beginning of freedom.

The end is the beginning of The Promise;
His Promise

Amen, Ameen, Shalom, Namaste.

The End   is the beginning

For look I am making all things new.

****

Crown of Stones: For You

Jasper, Sapphire, Chalcedony, Emerald, Sardonyx, Sardius, Chrysolite, Beryl, Topaz, Chrysoprase, Hyacinth, Amethyst.

The crown of stones are
For You
For your Love to be made whole
For You
For your pain to be healed
For You
For your heart to beat as one with Love
For You
For your thinking and feeling hemispheres to be joined
For You
For Love to conquer fear
For You, in you
For enlightenment of Love's Light
For You
For Love of God who is Love of others as self,
For You
A perfect measure made perfect; Golden;
For You
For mind, body and spirit to be One, joined, connected, whole (0);
One (1), I, (I), The' I Am'
Made whole again in Love (who is God)
In You, For You;,Self Actualsiation, Khudi
Only Love is One, Complete, unbroken
For you
Vitality; vibrant vibrations resonating positive energy for life,
Well being and peace
For You,
For You and for Others to be made whole in God's Love again.

Thanks be to God.

****

The Heavenly City

When will she come to be?
Zion: radiant with Love's Light
gleaming with gems of consciousness
of the promised land for healing pain
for 'All Nations', for all people
for the healing of pain for peace on Earth
from Heaven
                    to Earth
two fold peace doubled as Ephraim
within and without
above and
                    below
for Heaven to come down to earth;
It is His Promise;
this city radiant with Love's Light.

Please enter freely and bathe in her light
of minerals that Linus Pauling said
'you can trace every sickness, every disease, and every
ailment to a mineral deficiency'.

Just as Sulphur in homeopathy is relevant to every disease, so it is when Jesus Christ, The Whole Spirit of Love says through John in The Book of Revelation that sin puts us into the fiery lake of Sulphur;
cells debased as a six, six and a six, sick
proteins destabilised by cortisols of doubt.

Minerals and elements holding sacred geometrical forms
turning a hexagon into an octagon
                    (as seen in many ecclesiastical tiles)
Mans' imperfection made whole
transformed to an infinite flow of eights

****

for perfecting the flow for Love to flow freely
as a river of Gold
Eights: upright infinities of endorphin blood
offering a new blueprint for eternal life
of the spirit made whole with Our Fathers' Love
where spirit will not be cracked or broken but
'will reach the height of Everest' and beyond;
perhaps the true Kohinoor;
The true 'Mountain of Light'.

Amen, Ameen, Shalom, Namaste.

****

Notes and Reflections

Some space for your thoughts and feelings:

What fears do you want to conquer with Love?
Where are your stresses?
What negative emotion are you holding on to?

Place your hands across your forehead and focus on the fears and observe them melt away into conscious reason and a release of their restraints on Love to allow peace and healing .

This is a constant process of re newel of the self to maintain a positive spirit and transform from persistent stress to Peace and Love.

We call this ESR - Emotional Stress Release and I learned it from the Touch for Health Manual by Dr John Thie - another of my Bibles. Astounding knowledge of how our bodies work for the lay person and professional.

****

It can also be soothing to add in one drop of essential oil like Frankincense or Rose or Lavender or Jasmine diluted in a natural carrier oil when done at night (as long as you are not allergic and keep away from sunlight and your eyes). Also nice if a partner or friend can do for you. Sometimes there may be tears but do not hold them back for Jesus said ' Blessed/ Happy are those who mourn for they will be comforted.' Matthew 5:4

The grieving process is essential for healing the pain of loss, 'death is the last enemy'. I know this is true!

You could also add a crystal with consciousness in accord with The New Jerusalem aspect of Healing of course. Stress maybe work, person, grief, anger, lack of confidence, pain, tiredness, loss of energy, too much to do, conflict, jealousy, regret, envy, hatred, excess alcohol, drugs, stimulants, betrayal, divorce, loss, loss of everything, move, country culture, financial, death, abuse, violence, restrictions, control, relationship difficulties, many more things, too many to name.

****

Emotional Stress Processing Procedure

Stress - name one at a time and write how it affects your life.

....

....

....

....

Pain Level before ESR 1 2 3 4 5 6 7 8 9 10
Please circle

Pain Level after ESR 1 2 3 4 5 6 7 8 9 10
Please circle

Feelings now ....

....

....

....

....

....

....

....

....

Maybe worry has gone, more comfortable, less pain, not a problem, can cope with sorting out, more confident, happier, easier, more joy, more understanding, doesn't matter anymore. Always good to clarify and I always thank God.
Please copy and share.
Repeat for each pain or discomfort.

****

Emotional Stress Processing Procedure

Stress - name one at a time and write how it affects your life.

....

....

....

....

Pain Level before ESR 1 2 3 4 5 6 7 8 9 10
Please circle

Pain Level after ESR 1 2 3 4 5 6 7 8 9 10
Please circle

Feelings now ....

....

....

....

....

....

....

....

....

Maybe worry has gone, more comfortable, less pain, not a problem, can cope with sorting out, more confident, happier, easier, more joy, more understanding, doesn't matter anymore. Always good to clarify and I always thank God.
Please copy and share.
Repeat for each pain or discomfort.

****

Emotional Stress Processing Procedure

Stress - name one at a time and write how it affects your life.

....

....

....

....

Pain Level before ESR 1 2 3 4 5 6 7 8 9 10
Please circle

Pain Level after ESR 1 2 3 4 5 6 7 8 9 10
Please circle

Feelings now ....

....

....

....

....

....

....

....

....

Maybe worry has gone, more comfortable, less pain, not a problem, can cope with sorting out, more confident, happier, easier, more joy, more understanding, doesn't matter anymore. Always good to clarify and I always thank God.
Please copy and share.
Repeat for each pain or discomfort.

****

Emotional Stress Processing Procedure

Stress - name one at a time and write how it affects your life.

....

....

....

....

Pain Level before ESR 1 2 3 4 5 6 7 8 9 10
Please circle

Pain Level after ESR 1 2 3 4 5 6 7 8 9 10
Please circle

Feelings now ....

....

....

....

....

....

....

....

....

Maybe worry has gone, more comfortable, less pain, not a problem, can cope with sorting out, more confident, happier, easier, more joy, more understanding, doesn't matter anymore. Always good to clarify and I always thank God.
Please copy and share.
Repeat for each pain or discomfort.

****

Emotional Stress Processing Procedure

Stress - name one at a time and write how it affects your life.

....

....

....

....

Pain Level before ESR 1 2 3 4 5 6 7 8 9 10
Please circle

Pain Level after ESR 1 2 3 4 5 6 7 8 9 10
Please circle

Feelings now ....

....

....

....

....

....

....

....

....

Maybe worry has gone, more comfortable, less pain, not a problem, can cope with sorting out, more confident, happier, easier, more joy, more understanding, doesn't matter anymore. Always good to clarify and I always thank God. Please copy and share.
Repeat for each pain or discomfort.

****

****

****

****

Printed in Poland
by Amazon Fulfillment
Poland Sp. z o.o., Wrocław